JULIET

JULIET

A LIFE IN MEMORIES

Edited by
Georgiana Campbell

Sickle Moon Books
London

First published in 2017 by Sickle Moon Books, part of
Eland Publishing Ltd, in association with Fynn Crawley Vergos
and Lettice Crawley Peck

ISBN 978 1 903651 06 3

Cover image: *Juliet*
Back cover: *Juliet with unknown Afghan*

Text set in Great Britain by James Morris

Printed by Clays Ltd, St Ives Plc

CONTENTS

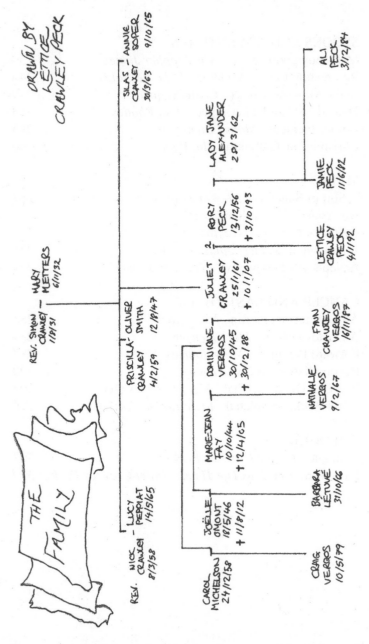

DRAWN BY LETTICE CRAWLEY PECK

THE FAMILY

Editor's Note
Georgiana Campbell

When Fynn, Lettice and I first discussed the idea of producing a volume to mark the tenth anniversary of their mother's death, we were unsure what form it should take. Juliet hardly seemed to have thrown a piece of paper away. The boxes of documents – bills and receipts, letters, and the diaries that she wrote almost every day of her adult life – filled half my sitting room.

With only fourteen months until January 2017, a full-length biography was out of the question. We settled on a collection of memories, best described by Fynn as 'a tribute to her life, based on experiences and relationships of those who were lucky, or sometimes unlucky, to know her'.

When we first contacted friends of Juliet's, some objected. They said that she would have hated the idea. It may have been that they were wary of a hagiography; they may have been worried that it might turn out to be a competition as to who owned Juliet.

Fynn's candour captures something that we, and particularly he and Lettice, felt: although Juliet's extraordinary and often tragic life seemed – and sometimes was – glamorous, she was not a saint, and this book does not attempt to portray her as one.

The format itself does raise difficulties. There are, inevitably, periods of her life which are not covered; there is a lack of a chronological narrative; some stories are repeated, and those that are sometimes contradict each other. To my mind, these lacunae occur in any biography; the collection of memories that we opted for merely highlights rather than glosses them over.

At times, delving into Juliet's life at such an intimate level has made me feel intrusive, even prurient, particularly when reading her diaries during the most sensitive and tragic moments of her life.

Like everyone else who has contributed to this book, I too adored Juliet. I filched her as a friend from my father, and enjoyed many an exotic or equine adventure with her subsequently. Her nose for cant, her elegance even in the most extreme conditions (16,000-foot Afghan passes included), her ability to giggle despite overwhelming tragedy were all sometimes intimidating, but mostly were utterly beguiling.

Juliet's friends and family have been extremely generous to contribute such frank and at times very personal recollections. As those who knew her extremely well have pointed out, intimacy often makes putting memories down on paper more rather than less taxing.

When the project was first mooted, we thought that we might receive a couple of dozen contributions. By mid-summer 2016, we had sixty-three. It was overwhelming and wonderful but, inevitably, some pieces overlapped too much. Editorial decisions were difficult. Thank you to all who have contributed pieces, whether they are included in this publication or not.

Barnaby and Rose Rogerson entrusted me, an editorial tyro, to collate a book with Eland's name on it, an extraordinarily generous gesture, or more probably, a testament to a true friendship with Juliet. Fynn and Lettice handed me an intriguing project, and I am hugely honoured to have been part of it. There would not be a book without my husband Mouse, who has corrected my more egregious errors of grammar and judgement, and who also has learnt to shop and to put up with a lot of soup.

Foreword

Fynn Crawley Vergos

'Bugger! Bugger! BUGGER!' Three words exclaimed in frustration through gritted teeth. Invariably they would follow the receipt of an oh-so-predictable bill, annoying long answerphone message (usually about a bill) or the discovery of a shredded parcel comprehensively destroyed by 'THAT BLOODY DOG!' Whatever the scenario, one could be sure that my mother was angry and certainly not to be approached without an antidote large cup of Earl Grey, or better still, a glass of wine.

My mother was not afraid to voice her opinions. There were so many of them.

Hers was a particularly rigorous style of parenting. Even now I can hear her passionate exclamations of fury. The wrath at Letty or me for disturbing her talking to an old friend in her drawing-room sanctuary. This was an absolute no-go area for little children and just not worth being caught alive trespassing in or despoiling with toys when she was away. We, of course, did both – just to irritate her. Pain; it was purely a concept. Incidents involving falling off a horse, donkey or camel, out of a tree or a sibling scrap were barely registered, or drowned out by the turning up of The Archers or Nina Simone. Outrage at some soppy scene or moment of weakness in a film or chick-flick would provoke an outcry of 'Oh yuck!' or 'Pathetic!' or 'Quick! Close your eyes!' The result: one should not be caught kissing girls – my poor excuse for not getting on the gravy train as soon as I would have liked.

Value and etiquette were schooled early on. She is still the voice of conscience on my shoulder, whispering in my ear that I have been too slow getting out of my seat to make way for a lady or pensioner on the tube; fuming that I have stacked the plates whilst clearing the table – hoi polloi; frustrated that I have not regularly topped up a wine glass to the three-quarter mark, irrespective of whether the person wants it or not (although as a victim, you probably don't remember this): '*Darling*, they should not feel the need to ask for more!'

The year 2017 marks the tenth anniversary of my mother's death. Even though it has been a decade since she lost her thirteen-year fight with cancer, I am always in awe of the number of people who, like me, have been shaped by her. Over the years many have introduced themselves to me as her friends, colleagues or acquaintances. Each one has a different story to tell that adds a piece to the vivid mosaic that was her life. There are so many of these, be it careering across a stubble field or distant mountain valley on a suitably unsuitable horse; snorting with casual but withering indignation mid-dinner party at some ill-thought-out statement; commandeering a tank and using it to get relief supplies into a besieged and ravaged city; or campaigning vociferously for what she thought was right, either in local elections, countryside marches or over a shop counter. Or, more simply, it could be running after her wild dogs as they chase and try to catch yet another cat in full view of the much villainised, but I fear misunderstood, 'corner cottage lady'. The stories go on and on. They have embedded themselves into a swashbuckling tale of adventure, compassion and courage, mischief and tomfoolery.

It is therefore unsurprising that not long after her death, I realised an account of her life had to be written. I had been to dinner with Bruce Wannell at his flat in York. We had been talking about my father, Dominique, and the circumstances surrounding his death. Of these there are different versions, official as well as unofficial. Nevertheless, Bruce had very kindly offered to write me an account of his memories surrounding the event: for this I will always be hugely grateful and have included it as part of this book. Even so, as I drove home that night with the stories of my father on my mind, my thoughts wandered and I started to think of my stepfather, Rory Peck, another man whose violent death is not free from ambiguity. I was captivated by the lives that these two men had led. Their stories reminded me of the tales that I had read about from the Great Game – daring characters like Alexander Burns, Arthur Connelly or Francis Younghusband who had risked everything on the hunt for information and adventure hidden in inaccessible and hostile territories. I realise now that occasional parallels can also be drawn to the reprobate Harry Flashman; although clearly they were no cowards. Even so, these two men – for all their faults – had displayed incredible daring and lived extraordinary lives, their exploits being recorded in books by admiring friends and colleagues.

Yet I realised that the one golden thread running through both of those lives, tying them together, was my mother. Hers was a life not on the touchline, but alongside her husbands: either in the center of intrigue in Pakistan, or in the mud and grime of whatever hellish conflict had taken their fancy. All this she achieved whilst maintaining her elegance, a trick she excelled in and which became her trademark. Purple feather or leopard print Emma Hope shoes were always magically clean – be it tramping across the Hindu Kush, mucking out the stables or climbing a tree to interview protesting environmental activists chained to its branches; all with me in tow I hasten to add.

This thread weaved itself through the tempestuous lives of these men and without it theirs would undoubtedly have been less vibrant. After the deaths of my fathers these experiences continued to define her lifestyle, and the thread snaked on through more intrigue, pain and adventure. By following this golden trail, we uncover the incredible and fascinating life that my mother led and can celebrate it for the extraordinary story that it is.

It would be easy to write about her as a Gertrude Bell-like character or a daring adventurer who liked 'dangerous men and more dangerous horses', as one obituary writer put it. Yet, as I meet more and more people who knew her, it becomes clearer to me that one of the most important attributes of my mother was the impact she had on such a wide variety of people. She lived so many different lives, not in succession but simultaneously, through her forty-five years (twenty one if she's reading this). She mixed with aristocrats and homeless orphans, terrorists and aid workers, rural folk and fast city types, religious conservatives and liberal secularists, artists and scientists, spies and politicians. As a result people were often only exposed to one aspect of her life. This is what I have been keen to address; to dispel some of the more grandiose myths, since people can be surprised to hear stories that paint her in stark contrast to the woman that they knew. People like their version of her.

Nevertheless, there is another and ultimately more significant reason for wanting to put together a story about her; so far, I have hinted at adoring friends, dashing husbands and outrageous stories. It is after all hard not to – one can easily romanticise such a life. For me it is different though, as what I saw and am often reminded of is a life of pain, loss, struggle and most of all loneliness. My mother left an astonishing and often illegible set of diaries, an almost unbroken account of her life from the age of sixteen until just before she died. She had terrible handwriting, and wrote when tired, late at night and often after having thoroughly enjoyed a far-from-teetotal dinner. These are fascinating but painful works; exposing the deepest emotions that she kept hidden from family, friends and public alike. Two husbands killed by gunfire. Thirteen years of battling with cancer and trying to keep it hidden to protect her children and loved ones. Constant financial difficulties. Deeply fractured relationships between friends and family. Questioning the very core of her Christian faith. Arguments and legal battles. Miscarriages. Physical deformity. Work based on lying and deceit in direct contradiction to her own moral sensibilities. But why catalogue such a grim and horrible list? The aim of this book is not to expose her vulnerability by laying bare her life for all to see. Rather is it something simple: to display the vivid and fantastic diversity of relationships she made over too short a life. It is expose more of the reality and less of the hyperbole that surrounds her. In truth my mother was not perfect – no one ever is – and the life she led was often far from glamorous. Yet even through all of this turmoil and strife she touched those around her with kindness and love. Maybe not all the time, but she made a damn good effort to do so. For me it is a reminder that when your chips are down the fight isn't over.

There are only a few phrases of hers where I can still hear her voice clearly in my head. There is one that sums her up for me. She reserved it for moments when it was just us, discussing some of the issues above, as we would often do on the long car journeys to and from school. Putting aside the dismissive bluster that was part of her act, she would give me a simple 'Chin up, darling'. It is this soft, tender and ultimately vulnerable person whom I remember and love. She was far more to me than my mother (and here I can hear a reverberating 'Yuck!'). She was my companion and friend; the person who needed my help and who asked my advice; the person whom I helped from an early age and then looked after even though she acted like the strongest person in the world. Ultimately she was just a young woman, with two small children as her closest support; and she absolutely nailed it.

THE EARLY YEARS

She Just Knew What She Wanted To Do
Simon Crawley (I)

Simon is Juliet's father.

When Juliet was young, she was shy and you would often find her sitting in a window seat, half covered by curtains, reading a book. She would be fully involved in any fun that was going on, but when there wasn't anything on in particular, she was always on her own with a book. She read anything that she could get hold of, but at this time it was mostly adventure. As a teenager, her imagination was fired by the years of the Raj, and she became totally caught up with *The Far Pavilions*, *The Jewel in the Crown*, then Rudyard Kipling, and Clive of India. She was an avid reader throughout her life.

She used to get regular stacks of books as they came off the press, history books, biographies and hundreds of books on war. She was well versed both in ancient and contemporary history.

She was very reticent about some things. I remember seeing her once as a child at a concert, and the school choir was singing. Julie was brought out from hiding under a table. When she got up there, she looked desperately embarrassed.

All through her life, Julie had a great love of dogs and horses. My father's family were all bat and ball. My father had five blues at Cambridge – cricket, golf, racquets, real tennis and tennis. Julie was quite a good and busy hockey player, but didn't want to compete with Priscilla, who played lacrosse for Kent and Scotland.

I didn't have any contacts with horses, and never had a living with glebe land to keep them. During the school holidays in Kent, the owners of a local school kindly let Priscilla and Julie ride and groom the horses. It was very close to our house and they would ride regularly – it was a great time for Julie, who would have been about nine. My brother married someone who had an estate just outside Newmarket and they had lots of ponies, so they would ride them.

When Julie was little, we got a beagle pup, with which she made great friends. When she was about fourteen, before she went to Marlborough, she was determined to have a parrot. She badgered us until we relented and we got this yellow-fronted Amazon whom we called Titus. She was devoted to it. She would have it out of the cage and spend hours with this animal – you had to go at it for a week or two before you got anywhere. Titus would greet you in the morning with 'I'm Titus; what a good boy'. Julie didn't teach him to laugh, but it had a laugh just like her. Sometimes it was quite embarrassing. We kept Titus in the kitchen, where the phone was. Somebody like the headmistress would ring up if Julie was in trouble or sick. Suddenly there would be a peal of laughter from Titus and he would say 'What a good boy', followed by shrieks of laughter. It was damn right embarrassing because it was so like Julie.

She read History of Art at Edinburgh, and came down from there saying that she wanted to do a year's voluntary service. We were at Patterdale at the time, where I was rector. She wanted to go to India. A neighbour of ours, a retired colonel who had been in the Indian army, put her in touch with two Baptist missionaries in Orissa. Life was pretty Spartan there: certain aspects of that life didn't fit easily with her – one of the two ladies said she couldn't have coffee for breakfast, only tea. She eventually left the two Baptists and went to work with a Mrs Webb, doing rescue work in the south.

Mrs Webb was a widow of some means, and when she retired did the same sort of work as Mother Teresa. She would scoop people up off the streets and help them get going again – they might see a heap in the road, which turned out to be a boy, whose legs were so thin that they were down one trouser leg.

Julie fulfilled her year's Voluntary Service Overseas, and when she came back to England, nothing satisfied her other than the idea of going back to India to work with the disadvantaged. She looked around for a group of people who did that, but realised that she would just be in an office in London. Then she came across Afghanaid, which gave her a chance of going out there. Afghanaid was started, I think, by Sandy Gall and Robert Cranborne, and set up refugee camps and a hospital. She got herself posted as a field officer, acting as liaison with the supporting government and the people who were working in and around Peshawar. Amongst other things, she set up a team to drive ambulances. They had their own vehicles to go into Afghanistan, which was under Russian occupation. These teams would get wounded mujahideen out and into hospital.

When we got letters, Mary would take out the less interesting bits and send them to our children so our three would know what was happening – it was important that we were all in touch. The others were in the UK at the time when Julie first went out with Afghanaid: Nick was a banker at Barclays; Silas was in his last year at Marlborough; and Priscilla, having read theology at university, worked with a group of Christian teachers called Scripture Union. Julie was a good correspondent and they wanted to hear.

We didn't worry; we are not worriers. We just said to God, 'Take care of them.' They were, especially Julie, going to do what they wanted to do. Julie was quite strong-minded and knew where she was going. In the time that she was in the sixth form at Marlborough, she became more determined. As a child, she wasn't difficult; she just knew what she wanted to do, but wasn't loud about it.

There was a school fancy-dress party when she was about fifteen. She dressed up as a pirate, with a wooden leg that I'd made, a patch on her eye, and Titus on her shoulder – it was an absolute winner and a triumph. We of course didn't know what was to come.

A Sense of Greater Moral Obligation
Priscilla Smith (I)

Priscilla is Juliet's sister.

At home, my sister was always called Julie. In latter years, it was a mark of extremely close friendship if she allowed you to use this diminutive form; I suspect we felt that it highlighted our very different childhood from those amongst whom we came to live in later years. For as a clergy family, we found ourselves living as missionaries in a foreign land – though in our case these were just unloved areas of England. In the mining village of Cinderford in the Forest of Dean (our father's first living) we had a wonderful house and garden, but the surrounding community's incest and spiritualism furnished my father with challenging pastoral situations – and us children with real-life ghost stories of exorcisms. In Northdown, a suburb of Margate with grim housing estates, I am convinced that Tracy Emin would have been in the same ghastly Brownie Pack as Julie and I were. Then there was Folkestone, or 'Old Folks' Town' as my father called it, where everyone else's granny except ours lived.

Despite these unfashionable locations, we were proud of our father: he was extremely good-looking; he was a man of integrity; he spoke melodically and well from the pulpit; and he had a beautiful singing voice. He was not parsonical and had a great sense of humour, but life in a vicarage increasingly made us feel alien. Treated as outsiders by the locals because our house was bigger, by the others in the independent schools because we lived in unfashionable towns, by those who were in the church because we were the vicar's children or by 'unbelievers' because we were religious, every which way we were alone. We carried with us this sense that we were called to represent God, and this sense of Greater Moral Obligation lay heavily upon our shoulders.

For myself – outgoing and confident – this presented a huge challenge that I grew to love, enjoying the endless round of coffee mornings and church meetings where we were required to talk to old ladies and hand around cakes. But I suspect for Julie – shy and quiet, preferring the company of only special friends – these occasions were agony. It seemed that we were always public exhibits. One Saturday, Daddy suddenly remembered that there was a fancy-dress competition – obligatory for us vicarage children – at the church bazaar. Quick as a flash he found a wide roll of paper, scribbled a bit of Hebrew on it and wound it round Julie and me. We entered, and won the competition as the Dead Sea Scrolls. Julie was mortified and furious at such public exposure.

Our early years were very happy. We went to a series of small private schools where we were drilled in the three Rs, had happy times on the beach at Botany Bay and played endless sport in the garden. We had guinea pigs and a dog and Julie and I started to ride at the local stables, toiling the three miles on our bicycles to spend the morning grooming, mucking out and riding. She was an animal lover throughout her life, and when my two brothers and I left for boarding school, my parents gave her a parrot called Titus Agrippa that she taught to speak and laugh.

She was acquisitive and collected and kept everything – ornaments of horses, golliwogs, and cuddly toys; clothes (she persuaded Mummy to buy her an embroidered denim jacket, the first acquisition in her extensive wardrobe – she had sixty pairs of jeans when she died); and above all letters and books. She loved books, reading avidly from an early age, and was most likely to be seen curled up in a corner deep in a novel. She read widely and intelligently and stored away information that would enable her to converse with all sorts of people in years to come. At first it was Enid Blyton, Josephine Pullein-Thompson, then C. S. Lewis, Tolkien, George MacDonald, and then the inevitable Georgette Heyer, Austen, and later Trollope.

Aged eleven, Julie joined me at Bedgebury Park in Kent, where clergy daughters were given significant bursaries. My fees cost twenty pounds per term, but my parents stretched themselves to pay fifty pounds for her to join me. At that time, clergy were extremely poorly paid; I remember one lunch, Daddy remarked that he was paid less than the dustman who was collecting the bins on the street outside. They were lean

Margate, 1969. L to R: Nick, Mary, Silas, Simon, Juliet, Priscilla

years and we felt the economies harshly. Mummy was an expert at spinning out the small resources, which included making our clothes for us. She often made the same garment in two sizes to reduce her workload, an idea that backfired on our first Sunday at school when we were allowed to wear our own clothes: both Julie and I appeared in blue skirts with orange flowers, mine accompanied by an orange hand-knitted jumper and hers by a blue one. We never wore the same again, and Julie's determination to be different was firmly established from that moment onwards.

Julie was especially good at drawing in those who needed the comfort of God's love. It was perhaps the beginning of her lifelong desire to look after what our family called 'lame ducks', for Julie was intrinsically kind and compassionate. She gathered around her a group of friends of whom she took care in different ways. She was fiercely loyal, loving, and full of fun and adventure.

When she was very little Mummy called her 'Peepo', possibly because she would peep out from behind her thick hair, or perhaps because she loved playing tricks and 'appearing' from behind some hidey hole. Our childhood was filled with laughter and jokes and apple-pie beds. Her sense of humour was huge, her joke repertoire extended by regular loans from the library of *The Big Red Rock Book of Jokes*. (The title joke was: What is big and red and eats rocks? A Big Red Rock Eater – guffaws of laughter…)

Julie was always full of fun and she was the most terrible tease; she was merciless in that regard. Laughter was never far away from her and always at the expense of one of us. Her quick-wittedness kept us all on our toes. I suspect that later on, when this was traded for public school sarcasm, those for whom it was too near the bone kept away.

Worsted and Margate

Rebecca Wallersteiner

Rebecca Wallersteiner was three months older than Juliet and her best friend in the early 1970s. She is currently an arts journalist.

'And the eagle spread its wings and soared higher and higher, over the far reaches of the earth, circling snow-topped mountains, forests and deserts, looking down at villages, cottages and scurrying ant-like humans,' read Juliet confidently, then aged nine, to the transfixed class.

Almost half a century ago, I first met Juliet at Chartfield, a village school at Westgate-on-Sea in Kent, run by two formidable, elderly spinsters, Miss Ballard and Miss Bailey. Excelling at English and blessed with a vivid imagination, Juliet invariably came top of the class in English. Sometimes I have a flashback of Juliet reading her story of the soaring eagle which had even impressed Miss Bailey. In the classroom, in small classes of around twelve, we sat on wooden benches neatly around a long desk, rather like children in Victorian pictures. Every morning, we sang old hymns reading from yellowing cards, neatly hand-written, by Miss Bailey. My younger brother, Anthony, later a teacher and Headmaster of Stowe School and contemporary of Juliet's brother, Silas, looks back in horror to the 'Dickensian teaching methods' employed at Chartfield, which included 'writing alphabetical

letters endlessly in grids and learning to count with an abacus'.
'Juliet's brother, Silas, was constantly in trouble and tears,
(the ruler was liberally applied) and I have a horrible feeling
that there was a dunce's corner.'

Born during the last decades of the nineteenth century,
Miss Ballard and Miss Bailey were part of the generation
who tragically lost thousands of its young men in the
trenches during the First World War. Like many of their
female contemporaries they had never married (or perhaps
they were gay, something we never considered at the time).
The schoolmistresses lavished their love on the school
and an ancient, mournful-looking pet tortoise, rather
unimaginatively called 'Tortie', which ambled around their
vegetable-garden munching lettuce. Miss B. and Miss B.
seemed to own three dresses which they wore in rotation –
these were pre-throw-away fashion days. Their unchanging
clothes were made of thick worsted wool, worn in all
seasons, while at least we children had a summer uniform.
For the rest of the year we proudly wore grey uniforms with
smart red jackets emblazoned with the emblem of a spider.

To occupy ourselves during school breaks, we children
played simple games of hop-scotch, cat's cradle, tag,
marbles, or hunted for unusually shaped leaves or pebbles
to add to Miss Bailey's geological collection. Another
more thrilling pastime, hidden from the teachers, was the
telling of ghost stories, at which Juliet was an unrivalled
master. Vanessa, Piers, Gillian, Amelia, Dawn, Claire – we
all hid under our desks scared witless, as Juliet recounted
terrifying tales of angry poltergeists, lights flashing on and
off in rambling vicarages, ghostly grey ladies and headless
men. I've since drawn upon the themes and emotions
triggered by Juliet's sleep-destroying ghost stories for my
own spectral tales as Richard Ingrams's 'Spook-Writer' in
the *Oldie* magazine.

During school holidays, long afternoons would pass with us playing happily in the garden, inventing games and stories, or on the beach just behind our house. While the adults read, or gossiped, Juliet and I disappeared into a parallel world, sprinting in swimsuits along lawns and the promenade, past slightly down-at-heel hotels, waving at rows of pensioners huddled on benches, past 'Pav's', the beach café, and across the sands, the salt air noisy with seagull calls. Although Juliet was generally more intrepid than I, and almost fearless, we were both tomboys and our games invariably had an adventurous, explorative element. At low tide we would paddle in tidal pools and search for crabs and unusual shells in tiny rockpools. A favourite game involved setting up a missionary camp and gathering driftwood to stake in the sand the outline of our huts. There was always some rubble washed up to serve as basic furniture – boxes to sit on and plastic bottles for vases. At Juliet's family's vicarage home, on the fringes of Margate, we used to spend hours climbing trees, with her beagle (called Bugle?) yapping at our heels. Sometimes Juliet challenged me to complete climbing a structure, built by her brothers and resembling an army training course, in the tall trees of the vicarage garden. Her warning that another child had recently fallen off and broken a limb was not reassuring.

Occasionally, when my grandmother gave us money for ice cream (and my mother didn't notice), we would illicitly cycle the mile and a half along the coast to raffish Margate. Few children who hung out there in the 1960s and 1970s could forget the lure of the amusement arcades, the familiar rhymes of the bingo callers, the sad plight of Margate pier destroyed by a winter gale and the seasonal excitement provided by the Mods and Rockers who staged their ritual fights on the seafront every Bank Holiday. Our Mecca was 'Dreamland', Margate's local fun-fair, originally based on New York's Coney Island fairground and with a similar brash, electric atmosphere. At

Dreamland Juliet and I dizzily inhaled the exhilarating aroma of psychedelic-coloured candyfloss, frying toffee apples and doughnuts and listened to the piercing shrieks of people riding the largest roller-coaster in Europe. We enjoyed the frisson of being there and soaking up the fun atmosphere as we only had enough cash between us for ice creams. Unknowingly, our paths may have crossed with the artist Tracey Emin, a year younger than us, who has drawn on her memories of growing up in 1960s Margate and the lure of Dreamland, with its fairground rides and its vivid neon signs, for her art.

Having given the grown-ups the slip, Juliet and I would pedal along Margate seafront admiring the donkeys and Punch and Judy show. On our escapades we recklessly climbed the chalky cliffs pretending we were scaling Mount Everest, scraping our knees and elbows, and cycled for miles along the coast.

In contrast to rackety Margate, the swinging 1960s seemed to have completely passed Westgate by. Its sleepy, slightly shabby Edwardian charm had been immortalised in a poem by John Betjeman during one of his holidays. Occasionally Westgate was dragged into the 1960s when my mother's friends from London visited. The most exotic of these was Nik Turner, the lead singer of the rock band Hawkwind. With his flowing, auburn locks, ginger Afghan coat, similarly coloured Afghan hound and bevy of hippie chicks in tow, Nick seemed to my pre-teen self to be the epitome of male elegance. He reminded me of Catweazel (the hero of a children's programme of the time). Although broad-minded, Juliet did not admire Nik's looks as much and thought he looked unkempt. I suspect that she preferred a cleaner-cut male look – more like the Milk Tray Man in the 1970s advert. Friendly Nik was a great storyteller. Entranced, we children and his hippie girls sat at his feet on the sands and listened as he recounted tales of his travels around Europe and America with the band crammed into the back of his rickety van. It used to be parked a street or two away from our house, in front of his elderly (and conservative-looking) parents' house in Westgate.

More often, Juliet and I chatted to the elderly people, many of whom were war veterans, who sat on benches at the seafront staring out to sea. Juliet charmed them with her impish grin and interest in their lives. We both enjoyed hearing about where bombs had fallen in the village, who had been killed or interned and how the local golf course was turned into an airstrip. Digging for buried treasure at the corner of the beach we once discovered an unexploded, rusty-looking bullet which was hastily confiscated by the adults. Another vivid memory is first hearing the Beatles' hit 'Yellow Submarine' on one of our illicit forays to Dreamland, circa 1969, and that it impressed me more than Juliet, who worried about the wellbeing of the men in the submarine.

Juliet often mentioned there had been missionaries and eminent cricketers in her family and that she intended to follow in their footsteps and become a missionary when she grew up, as well as a writer. We drifted apart after we left Chartfield and although we met again a couple of times in adult life, I remember her best as a child. Although I've been lucky enough to befriend many fascinating people during my life, Juliet was my first colourful friend. Her taste for adventure and *joie de vivre* were infectious and unforgettable.

Toast and Monte Carlo

Helen Jacobsen

After twenty years in investment banking, Helen gained a doctorate and became curator of French eighteenth-century decorative arts at the Wallace Collection, where she is now senior curator.

Juliet and I were at Marlborough together, at a time when girls were allowed only in the sixth form. Looking back on it, I suppose that must have been rather a challenge – nine hundred boys and only ninety girls – but you would certainly never have guessed so from Juliet's demeanour; she was always as cool as a cucumber. Although we were in different houses, we met in the first days of our first term because we were in the same set for history. We both had a bit of a crush on the beak, a fabulous man who could only have been in his mid-twenties but who imparted to both of us a great love for the subject. Apart from history lessons we frequently spent Sunday mornings together, when, after early service at church, Juliet entertained in her study with toast and marmalade. This often morphed into elevenses and suddenly it was lunchtime and all we had done was drink endless cups of coffee and chat and gossip with two or three friends, listening to Arlo Guthrie's 'Alice's Restaurant' at least five times. She was always, even then, very self-contained and didn't seem to suffer the paroxysms of teenage angst or self-doubt that the rest of us did, but of course she must have – it must just have been that she was better at keeping it to herself. She certainly didn't let on about which boys she may or may not have fancied; but she was expert at teasing and for those intelligent enough to realise it, she was actually flirting with them rather brilliantly.

It was really in the holidays when she and I saw each other most, and the summer after our 'A' levels we had the best time of all. Liz, one of our friends from school, lived in Monte Carlo and extremely generously but perhaps rather rashly invited us to stay – her parents were going away for a few weeks – and we didn't need to be asked twice. The glamour of Monte Carlo was pretty strong in those days, before its reputation had been tarnished by tax evasion and Russian expats, so off we set with great excitement. Travelling to the continent involved catching a ferry; after that, a train to Paris with loads of other student travellers and backpackers. Not that Juliet was ever in danger of being mistaken for a backpacker. I have no recollection of what type of luggage she had but it was certainly not a rucksack. In Paris we stayed in a two-star *pension* off the Rue de la Motte Picquet, where we received our 'A' level results (phoned through from home) and met up with our fellow travellers – three boys from Marlborough. They had definitely not been invited to stay by Liz's parents, but thought it would be fun to come down to Monaco anyway. I'm afraid our set of friends was not very erudite or intellectually motivated at that time, just exceptionally good fun and rather more interested in playing music and hanging out, and the prospect of doing all that on a beach and in the sun greatly appealed. To be fair, Juliet and I then planned to go on to Italy to do a History of Art tour so we did manage to combine some culture with our extensive leisure plans, and I'm sure it was this that had encouraged our parents to let us go – aged seventeen or so – without further chaperonage.

Monte Carlo proved every bit as exciting as we had anticipated. Liz's flat was on a high floor of a block overlooking the sea, which was about as glamorous as it got for us in those days. Not only that, Juliet and I were agog at the Yves Saint Laurent towels and the acres of marble in the five en suite bathrooms, none of which were regular currency in the lives we led at home in the late 1970s. And it was in Monaco that Juliet seemed to break out of her rather strait-laced and slightly old-fashioned persona – at Marlborough she had dressed very conservatively in tweed skirts and boots – but rather to my surprise, she was the first to strip off on the beach and tan herself topless, sporting Ray-Ban sunglasses and not much else every day. Since she had the great figure that stayed with her the rest of her life, this was an ornament to the Monaco beach scene, which is not something one could say about the rest of us lying next to her. After the sun had set we would go back to the flat and luxuriate in acres of bubble bath with tall glasses of Screwdrivers in hand – such decadence! It seems so tame now, but at the time we thought we were the chicest beings on the planet. The boys, by the way, had less good accommodation – the first night they arrived in Monaco they tried to sleep on the beach but were arrested and told in no uncertain terms to leave the principality; Liz couldn't let them stay in the flat but managed to sneak them past the porter and they then slept on the roof of the block each night. She did, bless her, risk her parents' wrath by allowing them into the flat in the evenings, so after the baths and the Screwdrivers we would sit drinking and listening to music – in fact all exactly as we had done at school, but substituting coffee with vodka. We felt incredibly sophisticated.

And from then on, Juliet was nothing but sophisticated. She always had such style! After Monaco we went on to Florence. In between galleries and churches, we toured the endless markets but she refused to buy one of the many fake

Louis Vuitton bags that by then were making their way on to the street – even when she had no money she would always somehow acquire the real thing. In Rome we stayed with a church contact of hers in a tenement block in an outlying suburb. It was rather different from Monte Carlo but, with Juliet around, of course it was enormous fun. We caught the train to Venice and were dazzled by how beautiful it all was.

I loved Juliet for her poise, elegance and self-containment and the air of apparent languor that much belied the intelligence and determination underneath. All of that, and a biting sense of humour with a wonderful laugh, remain my abiding memories of a wonderful friend.

Rebel in Pearls

Rose Baring

Rose Baring has swapped travelling the globe for a life publishing those who do. She also travels through the mysterious inner recesses of her own and her patients' psyches in her work as a psychotherapist.

It seemed apt that I should discover Juliet living in Russia when I was there. And apt that rather than living in Moscow like the vast majority of foreigners, she was living in Peredelkino, a retreat from the city where wooden dachas sheltered improbably but cosily, like mushrooms, in the all-encompassing forest. Like Churchill's description of the country itself, she had always been to me something of 'a riddle, wrapped in a mystery, inside an enigma'.

Our paths first crossed in Nick Bunch's History 'A' level class at Marlborough, where the 'Marseillaise' was played at full volume on a portable gramophone, complete with detachable horn, to get us in the spirit for classes on the French Revolution. It took place in a corner classroom, which always felt remote from the rest of the school, and there was a hint of mild anarchy in the class. Juliet arrived at the school a term after the rest of us sixth-form girls, sporting a blue Guernsey sweater, a blue A-line skirt, and what would become known as a Lady Di collar and pearls. She seemed very far from anarchy – as traditional as you could get, in fact.

There were a couple of boys who sat in the back row, both cheeky and funny, with whom I'd become friends. They were irreverent, somewhat lazy, and offered barefaced excuses for failing to hand in their prep. One was a talented rugby player, the other an inspired painter, and history was not their priority. They brought as many scowls as smiles to Nick Bunch's face. I'd migrated to the middle row to sit just in front of them. When Juliet arrived she did as I had done and sat with the more conscientious students at the front of the class, but it wasn't long before she was sitting in the back row with Godfrey and Alex, flirting particularly with Godfrey who I realise now was as close as I had ever come to a natural anarchist. When I bumped into both of them at a recent school reunion, Alex was as charming as ever, now balding, and a home-counties businessman in a Savile Row suit. Godfrey was all hair and dishevelment. He told me he had been living high up a Welsh valley in a house he built himself. He had never deviated from his passion for painting and refused to have anything to do with the art establishment.

Juliet and I crossed paths regularly in the eleven years between school and Russia, and I'd kept up with the dramatic, adventurous and at times tragic trajectory of her life. It was good to hear that she was in Russia and when she invited me for the weekend in Peredelkino I was delighted. On top of the pleasure of seeing her, I'd long felt that the pollution in central Moscow was killing me. I leaped at any excuse to escape into the countryside.

I'd been living the life of a single Russian woman – renting a room in a communal apartment with six Russian neighbours ranging in age and politics from a Stalinist granny, through a once-underground painter to a twenty-year-old would-be businessman – so it came as a surprise to find myself in a recognisably British family, even if it was playing itself out beneath a Russian canopy of trees. We went for a walk after lunch and picked mushrooms, eating a large, ragged chicken-of-the-woods which was in a perfect state of ripeness, with our meaty supper. The dogs needed feeding. Lettice's nanny was going back to the city for the night. On Sunday morning Juliet headed into Moscow for church. So far, so normal.

But in the background were the horses, which Juliet had shipped with her to Moscow from Pakistan. Two were tethered in opposite corners of the garden, while another, a mare in season, was being kept in what I remember as a makeshift stable with a pair of rails separating her from the garden. The simmering sexual tension outside communicated itself from time to time to us inside in the form of a whinny or a snort, and on one occasion with over-excited, strangled neighing and high-pitched cries, when the stallion managed to worry his stake loose and tried to break through the rails to the object of his desire. In the evening Juliet said the horses needed exercising, that it would calm them down, and I agreed to accompany her after church.

Little did I realise that what she had in mind was for the two of us to ride the pair that seemed to me to have only one thing on their minds, which wasn't a quiet hack. But yes, I was to ride the stallion while Juliet saddled up the mare. They were skittish from the outset and never settled into any kind of rhythm. Though ostensibly on the same ride, we weren't able to trot companionably side by side, but had to keep a sensible distance between us. The stallion was spooked, and when we tried to cross a little stream at the bottom of a steep bank he point blank refused. Juliet and the mare were now at the top of the far bank and the stallion chuntered from left to right trying to make up his mind to leap it. A firmer rider might have done it, but I hadn't been on a horse for some time. Juliet shouted down to me to dismount and lead him over, which worked easily. But once on the other side, he remembered what he wanted and bolted up the bank, pulling the reins from my hands.

I scrambled to the top, only to see the stallion climbing aboard the mare from behind, with Juliet still in the saddle. A Russian family with young children had chosen this sunny clearing for a picnic and were staring aghast at the unusual interruption, all the stranger for happening to a pair of foreigners. A few years earlier a foreign voice in Peredelkino would have been deeply suspicious. It was home to many a prominent member of the Union of Writers, most famously Pasternak, whose novel *Doctor Zhivago* had been smuggled to the West for publication and who had won the Nobel Prize for Literature in the following year, to the fury of the Soviet Communist Party.

Juliet jumped off and we managed to pull the horses apart before they got too engaged. She disappeared into the forest, telling me to wait for a few minutes before following her back home. My horse was in a lather of excitement. I walked him round and round the green clearing before venturing back into the brown beneath the conifers. It was laid out on a grid, each avenue lined intermittently with stacks of logs, and it was only when back in the gloom that I realised I'd paid no attention to our route. All avenues looked identical, but I plunged down what I thought was the right one. A couple of times I tried to remount from one of the log piles, but the stallion would not stay still, shifting his hindquarters skittishly out of reach each time I managed to align him. Miraculously, I emerged from the forest not far from the house.

We laughed that evening over dinner, particularly at the expressions on the faces of the Russian picnickers in the face of such unbridled passion. But there was talk between Colin (Peck), Rory and Juliet over selling some footage from Chechnya, and planning their next trip in the days to come. Compared to the Chechen War, our ride was a walk in the park, and I recognised, again, that Juliet and I were made of very different stuff.

Looking back on our school days now, I think what Godfrey and Juliet had in common was an inner refusal to play by the rules for the rules' sake. Where Godfrey's was on the surface, Juliet's rebellion was hidden from view and rarely articulated, even when she was clearly ignoring those rules for the sake of what she felt was important. She was one of nature's rebels, a free-thinker, camouflaged in pearls.

UNIVERSITY AND BEYOND

Curled Up with Mills & Boon
Ishbel Macpherson (I)

Ishbel worked in corporate finance in the City, most latterly at Dresdner Kleinwort Benson, for twenty-three years. Since then she has held various non-executive directorships and works in her local food bank. She is married to Philip.

My abiding image of Juliet at university is of her curled up in her armchair in front of an open fire in her capacious bedroom in the flat we shared, a glass of something lethal in one hand, a Mills & Boon in the other and Thatcher, her doting terrier, curled up in her lap. The perfect picture of the model student. As an aside, Thatcher was the first and best behaved of a long line of appallingly behaved rescue dogs.

We were in 49, Great King Street in Edinburgh in the early eighties. The flat was a masterpiece of faded grandeur; it comprised the ground and first floors of a huge Georgian house. Three of us lived as tenants of Leslie Walker: me, Juliet, and Catherine Cairns. Juliet was in the huge old dining room on the ground floor, Catherine was in a pretty room upstairs and I was in the box room at the back with a bullet lodged in the ceiling. During the winter months the flat was freezing: I used to have to break the ice in my sink in the mornings to clean my teeth. We all wore of lot of clothes in the winter and only a few less in the Scottish summer. The furniture was scratched, chipped and stained, as was the wall paper, but we had a large, elegant hall with a sweeping stone staircase and a first-floor double drawing room, one half of which was used as a dining room that seated at least fourteen. It was the perfect party place and, oh boy, did Juliet and Catherine throw great parties.

We would all dress up for parties; I think we took ourselves a bit too seriously on that front. It was the beginning of the era of big hair and big shoulders. Juliet, though, had already developed her individual style and always looked elegant in a combination of Oxfam and expensive boutique goods. She had two eyes back then too. Her eye patch became so much a part of her later trademark look that old photos of her still take me by surprise.

The evening would start with cocktails, the sort of ones that take the enamel off your teeth and all sense out of your speech. Folk would crowd in, at some point there might be a nod in the direction of some nibbles, but basically it was

Juliet, possibly in 49 Great King Street, 1980–1

just pan-galactic blasters of cocktails. The noise levels would surge, the emotions would heave. Never would they finish before three a.m. and never before Rory [Knight Bruce] had picked an argument with someone.

Rory and Juliet were a firm item back then. Rory stayed on at University an extra year as part of the Student Union. He was energetic, ebullient, articulate, unreliable and with a waspish sense of humour. He was a bright light in a dark room, drawing many to him; he moved in a circle of noisy sound and colour. Rarely sober in the evenings, he was also a hostess's nightmare as destruction often followed in his wake. Juliet would look on indulgently until she thought Rory had gone too far, and then an arch of the eyebrow or a purse of the lips often did the trick. If not, a sharp 'Rory' would bring him back to her side. Her cool elegance never ruffled. Although sometimes Great King Street's fabric would rattle at the sound of their arguments. Their relationship was never dull.

It was Juliet who came up with the bright idea of ordering two cocktails at once during Happy Hour at Charlie Parker's in order to save queuing time when we needed to discuss the all-important matter of all of our love lives. Her advice was always matter-of-fact, to the point and coolly delivered. I'm not sure that any of us ever listened to Juliet, nor indeed anyone else, but we did so enjoy the endless dissection of our relationships, or lack of them. Oh the passion we all felt in those days!

I perhaps shouldn't leave the impression that our lives completely revolved around alcohol and parties, but a lot of it did. The Fife Point to Point, the Odd Ball and the War Blinded were highlights of the year. As I look back it feels as though lectures, tutorials and essay writing were mainly unwelcome interruptions in an already hectic life.

When Juliet wasn't reading Mills & Boons, or cocktail menus at Charlie Parker's during Happy Hour, she read History of Art. It has to be admitted though that her approach to academia was somewhat relaxed. Lectures before eleven a.m. were not desirable and hence avoided, essay deadlines were flexible and tutorials were where you met your friends.

As finals approached, life got somewhat more serious and we all seemed to deal with it in different ways. I recorded in my diary:

It was quite interesting to see people's reaction to exams. Claire did less and less work and panicked more; Piggy thought she was having a nervous breakdown, but it turned out she had gas poisoning, as the gas fire in her room was leaking; Catherine got more and more bad-tempered and snapped all the time. Most people worked like absolute vegs, having the odd 'crise' of hysteria. Annette had hysterics in her first exam and was given a dispensation to sit them next year, she was delighted. Horror, nothing would persuade me to go through that hell again! The only person who seemed unaffected by the whole thing was Juliet, she read Mills & Boon throughout and watched a lot of television. She got a 2:2 in the end, thoroughly undeserved...

From a Rectory to Bohemia
Charlotte Black

Charlotte started work in the City in 1984 and is now a public affairs consultant. She combines work with the arts, and politics has been a thread throughout her career.

I met Juliet in Edinburgh in 1979. We were introduced by our especially naughty boyfriends – mine Patrick Conyngham and

Patterdale Rectory Garden, 1982/3. L to R: Juliet with Thatcher, Simon, Nick, Priscilla, Mary, Silas

Juliet's Rory Knight Bruce. Rory and Patrick had just moved in together and their landlord was the ever patient photographer and editor of the *Scottish Field*, Roddy Martine – who too often had to wipe away our tears after the scrapes the two boys got us into.

Juliet and I were teenagers emerging from rather strait-laced upbringings, she from the vicarage in the Lakes and me from a convent school miles from any bright lights in the Highlands. While we may have been nervous about betraying our Christian backgrounds, we were equally pretty fed up of being good. So we were both drawn to Patrick and Rory's often scandalous behaviour, and no doubt became a constant worry to all our poor parents.

Rory and Patrick led us both a merry dance with too many narrow squeaks and ups and downs to mention – and thus began for Juliet and for me parallel lives of unsuitable consorts and hazardous adventures.

Hopetoun House. L to R: Catherine Cairns, Ninian MacGregor, Thatcher, Juliet, Nicholas Ayles, Charlotte Black

But wherever we went we found Bohemia a tolerant and happy place and I am perfectly certain that neither Juliet nor I would have swapped all the thrills for any of the dashing or more eligible young men who crossed her path during the ensuing thirty years of our inseparable friendship.

Rock Chick and Rory

Tinsley Place Lockhart

In 1980, Tinsley was awarded a year of postgraduate study in Scottish Literature at the University of Edinburgh by the Rotary Club of Amherst, Virginia.

I had no Scottish ancestry, hated cold weather and hill walking, and thought all Scottish men were either short with red furry knees peeping from beneath their kilt, or tall with greasy lanky hair. The good Rotarians gave me a stipend of £15,000 – a fortune at that time, particularly for a student – but I didn't know that then and overspent horribly. People thought I was rich and I found myself in an elite crowd.

Juliet's inner circle was, firstly, Catherine Cairns. Catherine and Juliet were a duo when I met them in their second year. Catherine read something arcane – applied linguistics, I seem to remember – which she tackled with gusto. I'm not sure what Juliet read – but she pointedly curled up in armchairs on a Sunday, staring vacantly into space, while the rest of us frantically finished assignments due Monday morning. 'It's a sin to work on a Sunday,' she announced. Catherine explained that Juliet's father was a minister, rector of a parish in the Lake District.

Both Juliet and Catherine were slim, not very tall, pale-skinned, brown-haired, very English, and very grown-up. They were confident, ironic, stylish and social. They dressed in the public school style (later made famous by Princess Diana and *The Official Sloane Ranger Handbook* by Ann Barr and Peter York) – high-heel court shoes by Raine or Etienne Aigner, skinny jeans, boyfriend cotton shirts popped up like Eton winged collars, silk scarves wrapped and knotted like a stock, topped by oversized 'V'-neck lambswool or cashmere jumpers. They were in relationships with louche young ex-public school boys (black brogues with corduroy trousers, battered tweed jackets and stripy shirts with French cuffs): Catherine was with Piers; and Juliet was with Rory.

These pairings had gone on for years and were like mini-marriages. Where I grew up, we were locked into our dormitories at night at the women's college and nice girls hung on to the pretence of virginity and practised vapid coquetry like Blanche DuBois in Tennessee Williams's *A Streetcar Named Desire*, waiting by the phone on a Thursday night to be invited on a weekend date.

The couples' solidity and their resulting confidence gave me the opportunity for deeper friendships, friendships that have lasted my whole life. They behaved like grown-ups, with drinks, dinner parties, house party weekends and holidays abroad.

Earlier, I had met another couple – students from England called Patrick Deedes-Vincke and Lucy Bucknell – in the dining room in the basement of a Brutalist university building, the David Hume tower, where I ate my cheap if not tasty meals. They invited me to my first Edinburgh dinner party in Lucy's flat – in the Georgian New Town where all the English students aspired to live. About twenty people flanked a long table set up in the drawing room. Across the table was a slightly pudgy, awkward young woman who was Patrick's cousin, up for a visit. Her name was Viola. After I'd tossed back a couple of glasses of red wine with Virginian style, it seemed perfectly natural to call across the table, 'Could the instrument pass the salt?' This cruel witticism was met with gasps of delight from Rory and Piers. They introduced me to Juliet and Catherine and said we must meet up again. I had entered society.

While sitting with the crowd at the DHT between lectures, drinking coffees, Ishbel Macpherson asked if I would be her flatmate. I was living in digs with an old Swiss lady, Simonne Gompertz, a brilliant, housebound former academic. I spent my evenings propped up in bed smoking Craven A (I liked the black cat on the label), drinking cloying Drambuie and writing in my journal. I agreed instantly. My new home had a grand staircase, tall ceilings and battered chic furniture in a three-windowed drawing room. Rent was reasonable and no one was fussy.

Our local was called the Tilted Wig. Ishbel never went to the pub, which was a great disappointment to me, being a Virginia beer drinker – but I consoled myself by keeping Ishbel company as she drank endless mugs of Nescafé watching *The*

Juliet, Charlotte Black and Nicky Hay at the Rolling Stones concert at Slane in 1982

Professionals and *Panorama*. When she wasn't watching television, Ishbel spent most of her time in bed reading one Mills & Boon after another.

Forty Nine Great King Street was the home and sometimes workshop of a divorced man in his forties called Leslie Walker, who was an engineer. (His former wife was the famous Scottish artist Ethel Walker – her little pointy shoes were piled up in one of the downstairs cupboards.) He had a life-sized picture – the one with the enormous ship's chains in the background – of Isambard Kingdom Brunel in his dining room. He had a single product, a logic analyser (two different gauge pipe connectors, screwed together in the middle), and a single American client. One summer, Juliet (and maybe Catherine) made money by working for Leslie, screwing the connectors together on his dining table.

Students from England hosted weekly drinks parties in New Town drawing rooms; sometimes there was dinner, other times people went out to the restaurants on Dundas St – Bar Roma, the upstairs New Town Wine Bar, or Bell's Diner in Stockbridge where you had to bring your own wine. While Juliet was with Rory, I believe he tended to pay – he was older, working as the employed student representative for the University of Edinburgh, and I think he had money, which Juliet did not.

Juliet was social, not boozy, elegantly turned out, always with a wonderful drawling speaking manner which elongated my name 'Tiiiiiiiiinsley' with a twinkle in her tone – and her eyes, as if she was laughing at some private joke.

Juliet was paradoxical with money – she was frugal in her daily life, with habits from the rectory, but she always had the best quality things. I'm not qualified to speak of her finances in later life. But I do know that once she was in a tough spot, and a friend gave her a couple of thousand pounds to see her through. She spent it all on a Joseph coat. Defiant? Probably.

She certainly didn't want to give in to the frugality of her family. And she was never needy. It wasn't exactly pride, although Juliet had dignity. It was bravery.

Juliet had her own style, making a virtue of her characteristics. The whole time I knew her, her thick hair was cut short and plumy, rather like that made fashionable by David and Angie Bowie, or Linda McCartney, but not so long at the back. Her hair added to her height, and the elegance of her posture and carriage. Juliet never slouched. She was very rock chick – cool to offhand, and effortlessly with the right people. Rory was also in the style of Mick Jagger – wiry, bright, mouthy and hyperactive – so they were a couple of the day, tapping into the zeitgeist.

In the summer after I had been at Edinburgh, Juliet and Rory came out to stay with me in America. We were with each other all summer. We visited my late father and his wife out in Southport, Connecticut, overlooking Long Island Sound (Rory and my father played backgammon while Juliet and I sunbathed). We then went down to Virginia where we were six weeks with my mother Katharine and late step-father, former baseball star Jackie Jensen, at their Christmas tree farm. Rory and Juliet slept in the best bedroom and during the days worked trimming acres of trees in sticky humid weather, slapping mosquitos and brushing off ticks.

In the evenings and days off we swam in the James River, toured Monticello and partied, as only Virginians know how to do. Rory's cousin, the Reverend Allan Maclean, came for lunch but was so overcome by mint juleps, he had to be delivered home horizontally.

One day working in the tree plantation, the foul conditions drove Rory and Juliet to quarrel with such ferocity I was in tears – Juliet taunted Rory (I can't even remember about what) until he knocked her down and dragged her along the gravel driveway. I begged them to stop. She just laughed, as her arm bled from abrasion, and taunted him some more. He wasn't going to make her cry, or win. After Rory stomped off and Juliet went up to a bath, somehow they made it up, and no more was said about it.

The last time I saw Juliet we were both staying with Ishbel and Philip at Connaught Square. That night Juliet and I caught up on our news, happy to see each other but now with that adult reserve. We each went up to bed. By coincidence, at the same time we both got into our nightclothes and took our towels over our arms into the hallway to wash before bed. Our doors opened and we both stepped out into the darkened hallway at the same moment. Juliet then looked up and saw me – she wasn't wearing her patch and I could see where her eye had been – not that I minded at all. I felt like she was my sister, my family – I would have kissed it for her. But she didn't know that. She shrieked and retreated back into her room and wouldn't come out when I tapped. She was gone the next morning before I got up.

University Days

Rory Knight Bruce

Rory and Juliet walked out for several years when they were both in their mid-twenties, and were briefly engaged. He is a journalist.

It is hard to imagine now that in the late 1960s that erudite, metropolitan and worldly traveller Bruce Chatwin spent two years in the monochrome cold of the archaeology department in George Square at the University of Edinburgh. That, in all his memoirs, he only wrote one line about his sojourn – how long it took him to get from his garret flat on the Royal Mile to dinner with the Marquess of Linlithgow at Hopetoun House – tells us a lot about the place and the time.

When I arrived at Old College to matriculate on 4 October 1976, little to my mind, then or now, had changed. It was perhaps a comic irony that as I was handed my matriculation card – 7619562 – the photograph I had offered for it should have been taken in that hottest of European summers, somewhere in the Peloponnese.

Edinburgh University then was not what it is today, something of a popular if academic playground, where public school English students vie for splendid New Town Georgian flats and spend their student loans as pocket money, punting on the Stock Exchange. It was dour and drunken, the alleyways charmingly frosted, in the Old Town and on that ghastly windy walk from lectures to the Pollock Halls students' residence where I spent my first year, with vomit and urine.

I wrote a play which was savaged by the *Scotsman*, made money from it which I doubled at the bookies' and had irregular girlfriends. It was not uncommon to be involved in fights which, on one occasion, had me for three days in the Royal Infirmary. After my first year, I left.

But I was not ready or brave enough for the real world, so the next autumn saw me return and share one of those gracious Georgian flats in the New Town. People came round, we had supper parties and gradually I made some friends. I was a student politician, journalist and publisher so was perhaps, alongside my barely concealed contempt for my camp if not queer and mediocre lecturers, oblivious to the changing makeup of the student population.

Suddenly, as if word had got round on some public school grapevine, there were 109 Etonians who came in my third year. With them, I suppose, trailing behind, came the public school girls.

One of these, with no obvious merit or contribution to make to the bear-pit of my activist life, editing the *New Edinburgh Review* and being chairman of what today is the successful Polygon publishing house, was Juliet Crawley from Marlborough College. I remember seeing her first in the Teviot Row waitress service dining room, where I lunched daily, standing by the door as I was going to pay my bill, surrounded by other first-year girls doing their Art History degrees.

What Juliet had then, and continued to have throughout her life, was good friends. She was neither impressed by my endeavours nor my oratory. She could not have cared less about, what turned out in the bigger scheme of things to be, my minuscule student achievements. When I was elected to a year's sabbatical at the Students' Association, she was the same slightly caustic and detached, cheerful, even-tempered person who had been brought up in a variety of places and vicarages. I don't recollect her ever trying to play sport or draw attention to herself.

What has been said in one or two of her obituaries – one of which in *The Times*, written by Bruce Clark, made a nasty reference to me which Juliet would have hated – is that she was at university in possession of a fox terrier called Thatcher. I brought her that dog one day, from the Edinburgh Cat and Dogs' Home in Leith, as some kind of sorry for a night I had gone missing.

What I did not realise then, but I do now, is that when you love a terrier, you store up only sadness for its departure. We loved that dog, and played out our own love naïvely, like silly little grown-ups, not wondering really about what jobs we would do or how you really make life work. That, I suppose, is the idyll and the things.

Juliet with Thatcher

I enjoyed going to church with Juliet, and it was through her and her family that I first set foot in Patterdale in the Lake District. Of her good friends I remember Catherine Cairns, Barnaby Rogerson and Andrew Spearman would also come to stay. We would all walk the fells with Thatcher, all weathers, sometimes trying to keep up with the Ullswater Foxhounds on foot. On Sundays it was in to St Patrick's, where sometimes I read the lesson, and afterwards played pool with her younger brother Silas. I never slept as soundly as I did in that rectory, in a bedroom known as 'The Best Spare'.

What Juliet was best at in Edinburgh was giving dinner parties. I cannot really remember who did the cooking or where we got the wine but I would give something for one of those calm banquets now, perhaps twenty-four in Leslie Walker's in Great King Street. There was no frost or fighting then.

Juliet, when I met her at eighteen, had never stayed the night in a hotel. This was another totem of her kind upbringing. But, in the summer of 1981, she persuaded me, for I am not a traveller, to go to America with our fellow friend and student, the American Alpha Kappa Phi scholar Tinsley Place. We left Grand Central Station for Charlottesville, Virginia, on an Amtrak train, Juliet reading me the bible in a boxcar like a Southern Belle.

At the tree farm in Scotsville where we spent a month, we would after my mowing work sit out on the porch of the white clapboard plantation house with a mint julep, or tyre raft the James River by moonlight. I am not sure what Juliet did all day. At the Safeway store one day I heard Gary US Bonds' 'This Little Girl is Mine', which said that holiday, even if our friendship ended more like Bruce Springsteen's 'Racing in the Street'. When we got back to England I nearly died and, after a week, awoke in the Middlesex Hospital, Juliet at the bed's end.

Somewhere in the alleys of my memory and the trunks of letters of my past are the barely decipherable missives Juliet sent to me over four years. From Ruth 1:16: 'Don't urge me to leave you or to turn back from you. Where you go, I will go.' I just didn't know where I was going.

Juliet was immensely happy at Edinburgh University. Whilst being and making us modestly aware of her family's clerical, cricketing and golfing dynasty, she had that crystalline ability to be her own person which would later forge itself in rough countries and war zones. I have no knowledge of but much respect for that.

When she broke her back riding in Afghanistan, she asked me to come and see her in the Whittington Hospital in north London. When Rory Peck was killed, I saw her again in London and interviewed her for the *Evening Standard*, the fee for which was seed corn for the Rory Peck Trust.

At Healaugh, I was always welcome with the peripatetic guests I had in tow. She revived her university spirits and luncheons, now accompanied by a collection of Afghan spears and Russian samovars in respect for her two husbands, fathers to her children. Juliet never courted but never skirted danger.

Sometimes, I think of her memorial service at St Bride's, an accolade which those of us who have written a million words aspire to, and some like me may have attended with some jealousy. She didn't really write a word in print, but her example has done more than that, and inspired this book.

To everyone who knew Juliet, there will be a story to tell. Years after we last were proper friends she would still go and see my father in Devon. It lighted the last years of his life.

Today I live in his house and farm his farm. A fox terrier sleeps at the foot of and in my bed. A picture of Thatcher sits upon a wall. I still read Bruce Chatwin and visit his grave whenever I return each year to the Peloponnese.

But there is a living legacy of Juliet for me. Three years ago, a young man came to my farm to work on the apple harvest, and he comes here still. His family knew Juliet and Silas and he plays in a Christian band. We speak little, but I sometimes say go early or pay him more than I should afford. And I am sure he wonders about this, as he cycles off, and I hold the terrier and remember.

Some people go on to conquer the world with God and good. I would just get stuck on a journey to Hopetoun House.

For They Were Also People of the Book

Barnaby Rogerson

Barnaby is a publisher of travel books and has written about North Africa and early Islam.

I have a number of strong mental images of Juliet. Ironing Dominique's tattered jeans while her handsome French husband threw a bowie knife with unfailing accuracy into a doorframe. The night my wife and I brought a bottle of champagne into a hospital in the London Docks, and watched her budge up to make room for Rory, her second husband, on her narrow bed. We were celebrating their marriage and her survival from yet another near-death experience on a horse. I think Juliet had broken her back and they were contriving to enjoy this unusual honeymoon. Listening to her reading from the 'Song of Solomon' in St Bride's church under a vast black hat at Rory Peck's memorial service: 'I sought him whom my soul loves; I sought him, but found him not. I will rise now and go about the city, in the streets and in the squares; I will seek him whom my soul loves. I sought him, but found him not.' She was now the twice-widowed Juliet with a black eye patch and on the cusp of becoming a living legend.

But my most enduring memory of her is right at the end of her life, supremely elegant in tight trousers and surrounded by male admirers, horses, books, projects and her two beloved children. She was back on some vegan-like diet, but otherwise on conversational full throttle, denouncing the actions of Shell in West Africa, for whom she had recently worked. Her young son was being directed to open another bottle, on top of a Nuristani chest which served as a bar, whilst her small daughter entertained our own two young daughters on a sea of vapid society magazines spread over the thick, red, Bokhara carpet on the floor. The walls of the sitting room were covered with Soviet art, the kitchen filled with metal-riveted teapots from Afghanistan and bowls from Central Asia.

Juliet was passionately supportive of our current venture, to set ourselves up as travel publishers, and was busy identifying potential customers amongst her book-loving friends, whilst churning over some favourite titles in her mind. They were summoned from her memory bank, then dismissed with a snort of amusement at their remembered failings. She knew what we were looking for, for she had bought an entire set of the Eland library when we first took over the business. She was the only friend to do this.

Our visit had been organised by her sister Priscilla, who used the excuse of a Scottish reeling party to invite us up so that we could spend time with Juliet. She privately warned us that this would be the last time. The cancer had come back.

Priscilla was right and so was her timing. Juliet would have loathed any expression of sympathy, let alone a whiff of maudlin duty from us. Families were there to cope with that sort of thing; friends were for quite another purpose. For me there was also a curious symmetry to this last invitation, for I first came across Juliet through my friendship with her sister Priscilla.

***

Priscilla was in the year above me at St Andrews, reading Divinity at St Mary's College. She was kind and animated and

I liked the way her eyes would crinkle up with amusement at the world, yet you could never get her to say an unkind word against a living thing. We were part of a group of two dozen friends who would instinctively say yes to any invitation to climb a mountain or attend a Highland Ball. Details, distances, problems of transport and floor space for a sleeping bag could all be worked out later. So be it the Perth Hunt Ball, the Northern Meeting or the Muckle Flugga, we went.

It was on some such mission, to dance at a ball in a large house in the Lake District, that I first met the Crawley family. I was one of many packed into the spare bedrooms of the Rectory at Patterdale. The Crawleys seemed an idyllic family, tightly knit, loving and loyal, but instinctively inclusive of others. On this, and a subsequent visit, we rowed out on the waters, we tried to follow the fell hounds, we swam in the rain and we talked passionately over dinner. Neighbours dropped in for tea, and then the sodden, muddy clothes were

The Rectory in Patterdale where the Crawleys lived from 1981–7

exchanged for ballgowns. Friends were shared by the whole family, in part because both Juliet's and Priscilla's male guests were packed off into a boys' dormitory and left to chatter companionably away into the night.

Another reason for feeling at home at the Patterdale Rectory was that, before becoming a clergyman, the Revd Simon Crawley had been trained to be an officer in the Navy. He knew many of my father's naval friends from his days at the Dartmouth Naval College, whilst his oldest friend, Jeremy Rogerson, a third cousin of mine, had attended the same prep school as well as going up to the Naval College with him. Even if you are not an anthropologist, you will recognise that the identification of such shared links – of schools, regiments and professions – is an important ritual of the upper-middle class.

We also had another shared bond of social experience. For they, just like my own immediate family, were the church mice of a large, well-connected clan of wealthy cousins. So although there had been years of real poverty for the Crawley family (which I think included a period when they existed in a caravan living off heated-up cheap tins of food), they were also familiar with great wealth, which I witnessed for myself when asked to a dinner party at the house of a great aunt of Juliet's, who lived in some style and authority outside Edinburgh.

The one thing that I did not comprehend was the depth of faith within the Crawley family. There had been many vicars in my family and I took churchgoing in my stride. Indeed, walking with the Crawleys the short distance from the Rectory to the church for evensong was a genuinely beautiful way to fill the late afternoon, with the raking light blessing the deep valley and hills. It could also be surprisingly lively, depending on how many members of the family, at hand to play the guitar, were at home that weekend. But after ten years of enforced chapel attendance at prep and public school, often led by agnostic headmasters, I had no inkling that these rituals could have any moral dimension. Nor had I an idea that the Crawley family – father, mother and their four children – all believed that the bible was an eternally relevant message from God. Or that the world had ultimately to be divided into two groups: a minority of the Saved, surrounded by a seething mass of ignorant pagans.

So when Priscilla asked me to share a sleeper cabin with her, 'as it would be such fun', I took this as a wonderfully casual and stylish sexual invitation from an older woman. The look of horrified surprise on Priscilla's face when I slipped off all my clothes as the train left the station made me realise that something had been lost in translation. At least I began to learn that some Christians even took their faith to bed with them, and such was our friendship that we ended up laughing as the train rattled through the night. When I told Juliet this story she looked at me in stark surprise, for here clearly was a man with absolutely no judgement of character. Then through the tears of laughter, she managed to ask me if I had ever tried to seduce Mother Teresa. 'It might have been easier.'

Juliet herself appeared to be the calm, unflappably stylish centre of a continuous emotional storm incubated by her boyfriend Rory Knight Bruce. She would watch like a cat as alcohol-fuelled wit, fiercely held opinion, sexual gossip and relentless partying swirled around her, but never quite took possession of all of her. I noticed that her eyes shone brighter, and her smile became all the more deeply buried just when the social anarchy of her friends grew 'quite impossible'. It certainly looked that way. To an impressionable outsider it seemed that Rory also loved Patrick Conyngham who was simultaneously going out with Juliet's best friend, Charlotte Black. I had heard of triangular love affairs, but never yet witnessed such a rectangular relationship, which intrigued me. The two men shared a bedroom in a large Georgian town house that belonged to Roddy Martine, whom they flirted with, fawned on, bullied and entertained. Rory and I had a similar enthusiasm for dancing, and developed an alarming routine, by which he would take a flying leap into my crotch and writhe around like an impaled ballerina. As an attention grabber, it was flamboyantly effective at the early stages of a hunt ball. Fortunately he was as light as a fawn; many years later I found out that it was mere camouflage for one of the most persistent and discreet womanisers of his generation.

Juliet was the only actual student of this group of four friends, the one who needed to get up in the morning and attend lectures in History of Art. Rory had been a student, had a year off recovering from some illness, but was now back in Edinburgh dabbling in politics and about to set himself up as a magazine publisher and journalist. Patrick recited his own poetry but mostly painted and, through his friendship with Craigie Aitchison, flitted in and out of the alcoholic hothouse which included Francis Bacon and the Colony Club. Charlotte Black had just started up a restaurant-night club in Edinburgh called the Engine Room, a truly wonderful experiment, full of boiler-suited waitresses, gantry cranes, loud music and chaotic bill collecting. Aside from Charlotte, Juliet acquired two other sworn allies during her time as a student in Edinburgh. They became her lifelong friends, unquestionably sharing their various homes, adventures and secrets with Juliet. If I close my eyes I can see the slim, wide-eyed, ever curious and energetic Catherine Cairns swirling around on the dance floor, while Ishbel Macpherson is best remembered reclining gracefully on a lawn and accepting another drink with that wonderfully gravelly, deep purr of a voice.

It felt like I was being immersed in the nihilistic decadence of a J. P. Donleavy novel set in Edinburgh, which at that time seemed to be driven by a lot of energy, cheap rents and reinvention. Julian Bannerman had carved Bannerman's Bar out of a subterranean warehouse in the old city where students, socialist-bloc artists, tramps and professors of Gaelic could mingle at the bar, like the B-side to the intellectual effervescence of the Ricky Demarco gallery. If I squint further into the background of those Edinburgh days I can also pick out the bleached hair, purple glasses, red oilskins and faded dock jackets then worn by such future figures of the art world as Kate Boxer, Hugh Buchanan, Andrew Nairne and Lucinda Bredin. By happy chance there were also a lot of hospitable landowner-students around at this time, and they knitted together the world of St Andrews with that of Edinburgh. Hosts such as Edward Baxter (the young squire of Gilston) and Andrew Spearman at Fealar Lodge organised house parties, picnics at the races, dances, shoots and cocktail parties often from their own generous pockets.

I can't quite remember the exact timing of events, but towards the end of Juliet's time at Edinburgh, Rory had begun to fall in love with a younger art student, the beautiful, talented Belinda Eade, but then became officially engaged to Juliet as some corrective act of contrition. It was Juliet who had to make the final break, for I believe Rory was genuinely in love with them both. But having met both of her subsequent husbands – indeed I briefly worked beside one of them – I think I can detect that Juliet was not repelled by the wild, anarchic, unfaithful streak in her boyfriend, but attracted to it.

**

Two years later, we worked together in the offices of the Afghanistan Support Committee, in a charmingly decrepit Victorian office building – a maze of stairs, passages and doorways on the Charing Cross Road. Juliet was fuelled by a clear resolve to get herself out of the British Isles into some real life. She was calm, efficient and perfectly capable of working all hours of the day without so much as a sliver of a yawn. She had already worked for a charity in eastern India for a year and had found it deeply rewarding.

67

Juliet in Cuttack, Odisha, India, where she worked with the Baptist missionary
Mrs Webb

But she had not come back as so many returning volunteers, swathed in the textile proofs of her travels and smelling of patchouli. Instead she was addicted to those baggy, stylish body sweaters in black and grey silk and wool that she bought at Joseph in South Kensington along with their scent. But although she looked and smelt chic, there was nothing else that was opulent about her lifestyle. She lodged with her friend Catherine Cairns who owned a narrow, red-brick, terrace house on Ballater Road, within walking distance of Brixton market and the Ritzy cinema. It was a vibrant Caribbean community, full of neighbours who hung out their washing, and hung out of their front doors of a summer evening, swigging Red Stripe and giving you the time of day.

Her three Edinburgh girlfriends had achieved a remarkably successful transformation from feckless students to highly capable women. I seem to remember that Catherine was working for Warburgs; Charlotte was managing her own Eco-Green fund at the stockbroking firm of Brewin & Dolphin; and I never could keep up with what Ishbel was doing in the world of finance, but it soon resulted in her owning a house in a Mayfair square.

Meanwhile in a cupboard-like office within our building, Juliet had tracked down a ticket agency which gave us fantastic discounts for theatre seats if we could wait until after five on the evening of a performance. Unless someone else was paying, we ate in the Café Centrale on the edge of Soho, which had pew seats around red formica table-tops. They served the cheapest plates of pasta, allowed you to bring in your own wine and tarts worked in the rooms above.

Juliet had begun by working as a personal assistant to the director, Romey Fullerton, who was rapidly expanding the organisation, finding funding for it and dividing it into two, a political pressure group and a fully accountable charity, Afghanaid. Her boss was a young Conservative MP, then called Robert Cranborne, who was also trying to create freelance film units to report on world events and escape the duopoly of the BBC and ITV. In the process, we were promoted from a dingy back room to a spacious place that had windows overlooking Charing Cross Road, boasted a secretary-receptionist, a meeting room and the smell of freshly ground coffee.

Juliet was chiefly concerned with the charitable activities, which at this time specialised in providing work for single mothers and widows in the Afghan refugee camps in Pakistan and getting British medical staff to work in Pakistani clinics, especially for the fitting of new limbs. There was also a scheme to deliver monetary aid to peasant farmers within Afghanistan, which had a tactical agenda: keeping them on their land, especially in the Panjshir valley, helped bolster the resistance. This sort of work necessitated meticulous accounting and the preparation of detailed reports, which were shared with the funders.

There was a near continuous round of conferences, so that the different European aid agencies could swap experiences, carve out areas of responsibility, listen to the advice of the academic experts and meet up with the various governmental agencies that handed out money. It was also a dating agency, with fourteen rival Afghan resistance groups, all being wooed by different charities. The resistance groups were ferociously competitive with each other but so also were the charities which aspired to help them. Like an amoeba, they would divide up on some point of principle and break apart to form two rival organisations. Whilst I was working with Juliet, I seem to remember that this was about to happen. The great breaking issue of that hour was the pay rate of the prosthetists, the professionally trained medical staff who could make, measure and fit artificial limbs. Should they get the current UK rate, an air-conditioned apartment, car and driver, or try to fit into the local society as a cherished volunteer? This became very bitter, personal and politicised. In the deeper background were various American funding organisations and bizarre right-wing pressure groups who waged imaginary war not just against the Cold War socialist bloc but against the Democratic Party and the liberal intelligentsia. But we also got to meet genuine heroes like Nancy and Louis Dupree and the resistance commander Abdul Haq whilst attending lectures and seminars held at Sandhurst, the Royal United Services Institute and the International Institute for Strategic Studies.

Journalists and aid workers were fêted with our fine office coffee and de-briefed by Julian Gearing, who wrote up press releases and stories for our supporters' magazine. There was a constant flow of ambitious and maverick young men passing through – Peter Jouvenal, Edward Girardet, John

Gunston, James Blount, Guy Munthe, Peregrine Hodson, Guy Clutterbuck, Rory Peck and Bruce Wannell. They were either hoping to cut their teeth as freelance reporters, to get themselves a book commission or a job in the Foreign Office, to command a regiment of Baluch irregulars, buy emeralds on the cheap or do some good in the world. Most of them were impressed and charmed, if not permanently infatuated, with Juliet, even before she moved to Pakistan.

In terms of publicity our greatest coup was to fetch a dozen wounded Afghan freedom fighters from an enormous American plane at a US airbase in East Anglia, and bring them by coach to London to be interviewed on television by Sandy Gall. It was all going swimmingly until I ran over a tramp in Leicester Square, who had suddenly bolted out of a large dustbin singing 'Flower of Scotland'. It could have been a bit of a publicity blunder except that Juliet intervened – and the tramp proved an utter gentleman, refusing to blame us and waving the coach that I was driving on its way.

Once healed, the Afghan warriors got rather bored in London, trashed the house that had been lent to them and threw one of their number out of the window. Fortunately we kept that story to ourselves, but it was an interesting awakening to the tectonic ethnic divisions that subdivided Afghanistan. Instead of getting cross we put them to work, visiting London mosques under the avuncular care of a marvellous bearded Afghan called Dr Amanyar, whilst the youngest and most prepossessing of them, a Tajik warrior from the Panjshir valley, would come with me on long walks, hand delivering our press releases to the newspapers and the World Service. He even assisted me in trying to persuade Christina Foyle to set up her own publishing house, which would begin with a selection of reprinted Afghan travel books.

Within a few months, Juliet had achieved her ambition of being sent to Pakistan to help run the Afghanaid house in Peshawar. And with her, all the charm, humour and fascination of the office left, like a candle being blown out. Instead, the efficient glare of an office lamp. Now, a couple of days a week, Sir Oliver Forster oversaw Afghanaid reports, which ticked all the right boxes. He knew the ground well, for he had been unfailingly obstructive to all non-governmental organisations, quirky charities and free-spirited writers whilst earning his knighthood as our ambassador in Pakistan during the Soviet invasion of Afghanistan. I think it tickled him that he had now become their saviour – and it got him out of his wife's lunch parties.

Juliet knew I had remained a friend of Rory and Belinda, but neither this nor any other misdemeanour seemed to irritate her. I experienced her anger only once, when I quoted a line from the Gospels. It was on a skiing holiday that we took together in this period, a cheap test-run of a chalet being set up by a friend of mine. Typically she ignored all the good-looking officer-types on this trip; the only man who attracted her interest was my dark, sulky, clever but difficult script-writing friend. I still remember how her eyes flashed with rare fire as she explained to me with icy clarity that she read the bible every night of her life, and had no need of any instruction, most especially from someone like me. I think by this stage of her life she had already developed a horror of people using the holy text in public to support their own desires. For Juliet it was something so important that she kept it as a private, compass-like jewel with which she navigated her own way through life.

No wonder she understood the Afghans so well, for they were also people of the book. And Juliet, like them, could switch between pauper and princess at the blink of an eye.

Rice Pudding and Cardamom
Eliza Meath Baker

Eliza is Catherine Cairns's sister and is a painter, based in London.

The time that Juliet, Catherine and I lived in Catherine's house in Brixton was probably the least eventful of her life: a bridge between her Gatsbyesque years at Edinburgh University and her real life abroad. She was working for the Afghanistan Support Committee, weathering the end of an engagement and the fall from grace that is your first adult job. I remember her then as being serious but teasing, and even then she always moved as though she were stiff and weary.

So I don't have interesting stories to tell you from Ballater Road, but I can see her in three things she left behind: Thatcher, her angry terrier; Mohammed Hashim Saad, an Afghan mujahideen; and knife holes in the kitchen door.

Juliet rescued Thatcher from Edinburgh Dogs' Home, and they were always together. He is inextricably linked with my image of Juliet at that time. He was very self-conscious, and if he thought you were talking about him, he would sit with his back to you and swivel his eyes impossibly far round to look at you whilst pretending not to. He attacked men and motorbikes, and we speculated about what must have happened to him in his earlier life. I don't remember agreeing to keep Thatcher when Juliet went to Peshawar, but suddenly he was mine, and Brixton seemed to be nothing but men and

Dominique Vergos, Afghanistan 1980/1. Juliet turned this image into a card. In it she wrote:

> *Dearest Granny, I have three over-fed stallions in my tiny garden –*
> *regularly each night one of them escapes and jumps on another. The*
> *other night I had to send for my horseman at 2.00am to restore order. I*
> *have managed to cut my household and animal staff down to eight – but*
> *am worried about the garden because I still have no-one to work there. I*
> *have been offered two jobs – one as a PW to the Gigolo of Peshawar*
> *and the other as a consultant – but I decided it was safer to stay with*
> *UNHCR – even if I am inundated with work. I had dinner with Sandy*
> *Gall and friends the other night. He really is such a nice man – and it's*
> *always a relief to meet someone who drinks more whiskey than I do. This*
> *is Dominique in the 'Desert of Death' West Afghanistan on one of his*
> *incredible journeys. All my love, Julie x*

motorbikes. At Juliet's funeral, someone showed me that he had brought a photograph of Thatcher with him, as he thought he should be there.

Juliet was living in Peshawar when she asked us to have Hashim to stay for ten days following surgery to repair a gunshot wound to his arm. He stayed for six months. During the Soviet occupation of Afghanistan his mother and a brother had been killed when the Russians blew up a tunnel that their train was travelling through. This led him to the resistance movement under Ahmad Shah Massoud, and to work for Jami'at-e Islami in Peshawar. The day he arrived, Hashim, Catherine and I stood in Juliet's room, now Hashim's, and worked out the direction of Mecca. He prayed loudly and sang songs to himself about a girl he loved but could never marry. With him we met other Afghans living in London: suppers in bedsits, where there was never alcohol but always rice pudding with cardamom. I remember how these political exiles attracted a lot of quite pious and reverential attention, but mostly we just had a laugh together, which I think was revelatory for all of us – and we would never have met if it weren't for Juliet. Hashim was embarrassed when we hugged him and cried as we said goodbye, and after a couple of letters to 'dear sisters', we never heard from him again.

The holes in the door were made by Dominique. Juliet brought him to stay, and he was an alien presence with his grey mane and Cuban heels. As we sat in the kitchen having supper, Dominique kept flicking a knife past our faces into the door. Juliet was very giggly around him, and though she pretended to disapprove of the knife-throwing, she married him soon after.

From a Mouse to a Lion
Ed Gorman

Ed Gorman worked for The Times *for twenty-five years, including as a foreign correspondent. He now works as a freelance writer.*

The strongest sense I have of Juliet is of the remarkable journey she made in the short time allotted to her on this earth. My earliest memory of her is of a quiet, shy, softly spoken, mouse-like individual in tweed skirts and cashmere sweaters at Marlborough College. She was someone who was rarely seen and rarely heard in those days. I have a vision of her, fixed in my mind, walking down the hill from her house at Summerfield across the cricket pitches carrying her work files on the way to afternoon lessons in the sunshine. This was a young Juliet who very much kept herself to herself.

I barely knew her then and did not see her again until after school, five years later, when I turned up on another sunny day at the offices of Afghanaid at 22, Charing Cross Road in London, to find Juliet – of all people – occupying the role of office secretary. By then the ambition, the determination and the steel that would mark the mature woman that she became was already beginning to make itself felt. Juliet loved working for Afghanaid but she was intensely frustrated about being office-bound in London. She wanted to get involved at the sharp end where she could live among the people she wanted to help. 'I want to go to Peshawar,' was her mantra and I sensed even then that she would get what she wanted.

Cut to the North-West Frontier Province and there we find Juliet in her element, finally being given the chance to get her teeth into something that had become so dear to her heart. And that is why I talk of a journey and a transformation. Far from the early bashfulness, Juliet now hit her stride. There was a calmness about her and she had real presence, she could command a room, she was able to make decisions and bring good judgement to bear on them. And perhaps more than anything she was learning to thrive in the ultimate man's world as she dealt firmly but fairly with Afghan men (mainly) who came looking for help from Britain's only charity dedicated to alleviating the plight of Afghans. It is easy to forget that Juliet had chosen a pretty radical departure, swapping a relatively easy-going life in London – even if it irritated her immensely – for the drama and romance of the North-West Frontier and the skulduggery of the Afghan diaspora.

For me, a young freelance journalist from England with hugely ambitious ideas of covering the war inside Afghanistan, it was great knowing that Juliet was running things at Gulmohar Road. We had a familiar background from our school days and Juliet was always fun to share recollections with. She was intensely curious to hear firsthand what was going on 'inside' Afghanistan and we spent many an hour talking after my various trips over the border. I remember an impish sense of humour – Juliet was quite proper but she knew how to laugh at herself.

However well you thought you knew her, there was always a reserve about Juliet – she would let you in this far, but no further. I thought I knew her pretty well but I was as surprised as anyone when she fell for Dominique. You could hardly get anyone more different. This was opposites attracting at the extreme. Dominique was wild, unpredictable and a million miles from the culture that marked Juliet, the modest and unassuming daughter of a rural Yorkshire parson with immaculate manners and standards. Dominique could be highly intimidating and there was always a mystery about him that endured long after his death. What exactly was he doing out there … but also perhaps what did Juliet see in him?

I guess she was fascinated by extravagantly extrovert and noisy men, because Rory was in some ways quite similar to Dominique. Another larger than life and, at times, abrasive character who captivated Juliet, he was her perfect foil as they embarked on a life of adventure in Russia and elsewhere. I never saw her in her last years when she returned to England and set up the Rory Peck Trust but there was a stoicism about Juliet that I can only imagine must have helped to arm her in her last great battle. And of course there was so much more she had to give.

Eyes that Dance
Catherine Cairns

Soon after meeting each other in a lecture hall at Edinburgh in 1979, Juliet moved into Catherine's appartment in St Bernard's Crescent. They became, and remained for the rest of Juliet's life, firm friends.

THATCHER
About twenty-four hours after one of Juliet and Rory Knight Bruce's more theatrical rows (which often ended with Rory wailing all night on the stairs outside our top-floor flat), I was alone, mooching about in my room. Probably recovering from the party. Probably wondering if this time they would split up. I never heard the front door open. Who then should trot briskly and bossily into my room, but a small brown and white terrier with a brand-new collar trailing a brand-new lead. That was my first sight of Thatcher, who then became glue in the family. One thing of which we never cured him was his passion for attacking men's feet, especially feet wearing polished brown brogues.

PARTIES GALORE
Who remembers the Midsummer Balls at Hopetoun House? And what about the time when we all gatecrashed the Assembly Rooms, with Charlotte [Black] poised below to feign illness if need be to divert security. Scrambling up the fire escape in a full-bodied, floaty, freezing ballgown, struggling not to rip it in the wind, with snow whistling around us. And then those

fantastic New Year parties at Balavil, thanks to darling Ishbel [Macpherson] and her immensely generous and kind parents, Sir Tommy and Lady Mac. My goodness what fun we had, how very spoiled we were.

HALCYON DAYS AT UNIVERSITY

Wonderful walks and driftwood fires and Thatcher being whirled round with his teeth clamped to the end of a stick – with such a good crowd of friends. I treasured the weekends at Patterdale with Juliet's family and especially her parents, for whom I felt and feel great affection. With hindsight I know that the feelings were not entirely reciprocated, but it was some years before I learned about that.

And then Great King Street, what a joy it was to live there, in Leslie's house – shabby grandeur, Tom Collins and prairie oyster parties. Making logic analysers. Dear Leslie let us bumble away for hours with soldering irons, soldering

Juliet met Catherine Cairns at Edinburgh University, where they became firm friends

chips on to circuit boards. He paid us well – but only if our logic analyser worked. A cup of tea, or a glass of wine, lots of gossip and piles of logic analysers on the dining room table ... productivity tended to be a bit mixed.

SHOPAHOLICS

Auctions, junk shops, and then outrageous purchases. Dire extravagance in Corniche at Edinburgh – boding ill for both our years ahead – but also extremes in the other, frugal, direction: huge vats of lights cooked for Thatcher, and marvellous antiquated washing machines, bought at auction for a pound, with mangles on the top. They often overflowed, and we sloshed around the kitchen frantically mopping up as the dodgy wiring made our fingers tickle with little juddering fizzles.

HASHIM

Mohammed Hashim Saad, thanks to Juliet, came to live with Eliza and me for a while in Ballater Road. He arrived in London as a wounded mujahid, expecting tea and food on demand, quickly adapted to London life, and ended up ironing his own shirts and taking himself off to adorn drinks parties in Chelsea. There he would stand, clutching a large glass of water, tall and beautiful and robed, the centre of fascinated attention.

MAINE

Eating lobster and boiled potatoes. Again and again, lobster, lemon juice, boiled potatoes, butter and salt and wine. What a treat, lobster and friends. Maine with Rory and all the children, Maine just with Juliet. I shall never forget that first winter trip with Juliet, after Rory's death, chopping a hole in the ice on Clearwater lake to get water to wash and cook.

Six of us flew up to a lake on the Canadian border, planning to survive for a week off the land. How smug we were about how well we would manage – but we failed to catch a single fish.

I remember being so proud about finding masses of freshwater mussels – but freshwater mussels taste quite disgusting, like rubbery mud. We shot a squirrel and picked some raspberries, but one squirrel in raspberry sauce does not go far among six people. Then, Juliet and I heard a gunshot. We turned and pelted back down to the water. Moose came to graze in our lake at dusk and dawn to eat the water plants. A moose shoulder-height in water is not able to put up much resistance to men in a canoe – especially if stunned from a rather ineffectual shot in the forehead. Rory hopped on to the slightly dazed doe's back, grasped her by the ears and steered her to shore; then, as she neared the shallows, he cut her throat. She was our food for the rest of the week. I shall never forget the deliciousness of the liver, that first night. But imagine the butchering we had to do to conceal the slaughter, the blood slicking right out into the middle of the lake.

JEKYLL AND HYDE JULIET

Juliet had a sharp and sarky tongue. She loved to tease – it was something she did. Sometimes it was clever and funny; sometimes it could be rather tiresome and even unkind, especially after a drink or two. But that mischievousness was part of her character – hence why she loved japes. I was her willing if rather inept accomplice there. She was brilliant at thinking April Fools up. I still smile at the one we once played on Frank Houghton Brown [then huntsman of the Middleton], pretending that the RSPCA were after him; or spray painting graffiti on the roads at night in support of hunting – vandalism pure and simple, but fun to do – although I must admit not helpful to the cause. My role was to drive (rather badly; the wrong way) around the roundabouts, with Juliet hopping out with the paint spray cans.

WONDERFUL HUNTING MORNINGS

York & Ainsty South and the Middleton, how different each pack was and what fun they both were. Scrambling out of bed, making tea, tying stocks, replenishing our hunt flasks, setting off, often a bit late, digging out the map, and then, the meet and days of glory. Mark Atkinson, Master of the Y&A (S), helping us with beautifully polished and plaited ponies, such fun to go out with and always ready to give us a lead.

EYES THAT DANCE

After Juliet visited me in South Africa for the second time, in May 2005, she sent me a book called *The Man with the Dancing Eyes* by Sophie Dahl.

In her accompanying letter, she talked about watching Spencer [Crawley] play cricket in his last term at Harrow, which led her to write this about her dear friend and cousin, Harriet [Spencer's mother]:

> Harriet is remarkable – it is five months since she lost her great love – who had brought real happiness back into her life – and yet she is generally gay and positive. Always giving, always thinking of everyone else – and so much energy. What an example and inspiration she is to us.

All this she wrote knowing, but telling few, that she was ill again. What she wrote was true about Harriet, but equally well applied to her.

There were many men enamoured with Juliet over the years – she exerted a fascination over men that I have never seen rivalled. There were only a very small number of men to whom she was attracted and a much smaller number with whom she was truly in love. I think I knew all those she loved – there were very few but more than two. What I can say about those that I knew is that they all had dancing eyes.

From Joseph to Jamiat

Romey Poston (née Fullerton)

*Romey Fullerton ran Afghanaid's London office. Its origins were
in the Afghan Support Committee formed in London in 1981.
Initially its purpose was to provide emergency relief to those
fleeing Afghanistan and those in need of medical attention.*

When a young Juliet Crawley telephoned 22, Charing
Cross Road in 1985, she was calling in response to
an advert for a position in the (very modest) London office
of Afghanaid. Her voice over the phone was bright, she was
persistent and she asked some searching questions and one
got the distinct impression that she had already decided that
this was the job she was going to do. The resulting letter of
application was a bit scatty and her referees were impossibly
grand for such a straightforward post, but she had lived
and worked in a leper colony in India, and had loved it and
believed in it, despite having had quite a hard time. This made
her promising material for our batty little band of dedicated
enthusiasts in Afghanaid. At the interview, her combination of
determination and enthusiasm won her the day.

Juliet made an immediate impact on life in our little trio
of offices in Charing Cross Road. The volume and length
of phone calls went up and when I gently enquired (after
contacts had complained of struggling to get through) Juliet
patiently explained that her friends were used to phoning her

for advice about life's various tribulations and she thought it was important to support them. And the quality of the coffee in the office sky-rocketed. Walking out one lunchtime she had happened across a rather distinguished little coffee and tea merchant in Soho. She was intensely pleased with the discovery and was adamant that we should try some out. The smallest of nudges put an end to Juliet's role as agony-aunt during working hours, but nothing would ever budge her on the quality of the coffee, however limited the petty cash.

The early days of Afghanaid were very focused, very hand to mouth. The needs in Afghanistan were enormous and very pressing, and the knowledge and understanding of the situation was very limited in the UK, not much better in most of Europe and negligible in the States. We had our work cut out. We were very under-resourced and under-manned. It will seem ridiculous that, when Juliet joined us, there were just three full-time employees in the London office and only the most rudimentary office in Peshawar. All our lives were pretty much devoted to the task in hand. We were a happy bunch and, for the most part, remarkably, more went right for all of us than not.

Since its beginning, Afghanaid had worked hard at developing good relations with politicians, official contacts and the media to raise awareness of what was happening in Afghanistan – the needs of refugees and especially those internally displaced within Afghanistan. Contacts had been developed with the Foreign Office to the point where the South Asia Department (which deals with the Indian subcontinent and Afghanistan) would send all officers joining the department along to the Afghanaid offices for a briefing. Not long after Juliet joined us, we were expecting two such officers, the new deputy head of department and someone from a research department. It was a bitingly cold winter's day and very early that morning, Juliet had phoned, somewhat distressed, to ask if she could bring her fox terrier, Thatcher, into the office. Through her tears, she apologised and explained that she and her fiancé, Rory, had broken up the night before and that he was no longer going to look after Thatcher during the day. When our official visitors arrived, Juliet (bravely pretending to be normal though her eyes were still ringed with red) greeted them, showed them through and offered them coffee. Thatcher had been secreted in the third office, but when Juliet opened the door to bring the coffee, Thatcher, ever an enthusiast, shot through the crack in the door, then leapt on to my knee, the better to view our visitors. It was so cold that us staff were sitting wearing fingerless gloves and scarves. Our visitors never took their coats off. Greatly to their credit, they ignored Thatcher, stayed over an hour and asked many questions. (It may not be a coincidence that, not long afterwards, the Foreign Office thought we might benefit from a grant towards our Information Service.)

As our activities grew, we attracted numerous part-time volunteers, including barristers and former British ambassadors. Afghanaid was extremely fortunate in having Robert Cranborne as its chairman, plus a very able and supportive board of trustees who helped us to gain access to the parliaments, foreign ministries and aid departments in London and overseas. By the time Juliet joined us, we had won the initial battle to persuade governments to fund cross-border food aid and basic agricultural aid to the embattled and isolated communities in the valleys and mountains of Afghanistan. Afghanaid had played its part in winning that battle and was rewarded with substantial funding. However, we had much to do to set up the structures that would allow us to turn initial aid deliveries into a regular programme of sustained, responsive and accountable aid. Most of the European aid agencies working in Afghanistan were in the same boat (although the French medical aid organisations like

Médecins Sans Frontières and Aide Médicale Internationale had a longer experience of working in many areas of the country). We all gained enormously from twice-yearly international conferences discussing the challenges and sharing best practice as well as from the six-weekly European co-ordinating meetings. As new countries started their own aid or support groups, it was important to draw them in. Norway was one such country and the first time I saw Juliet truly come alight with a task was when I asked her to make contact with this newly formed group and find out all about it and then, if possible, support and involve it. It may have been the prospect of a trip overseas (a prospect which always stirred Juliet's blood) or it may simply have been owning a task entirely which she also always enjoyed.

Juliet would never take time off if life went pear-shaped. But, naturally, standards had to be maintained: one early stipulation to her employment was that she would need to be off for the first day of any Joseph sale. Was that what was behind her ability to make even a tweed jacket with a hole in it look stylish?

Finding the right person to go out to work in the office in Peshawar was always a challenge. Life on the North-West Frontier is wonderful and exciting, but not for everyone. The stresses of living in a very different culture, without many of the creature comforts we are used to in the West, can cause weak spots in a personality to crack open. Too many hippies had made their way through Afghanistan and Pakistan for young Western foreigners to be viewed with unalloyed admiration and ex-pat life can all too easily distract one from the real task of getting to understand the locals and, most importantly for us, the Afghans. Setting up and running aid programmes in a way that builds the recipient community's self-reliance needs acute listening skills combined with cultural sensitivity.

Juliet had always wanted to be posted out to Peshawar – it was one of the questions she had asked during that first telephone conversation. She needed to work in the London office for a spell to understand the pressures and requirements from that end, but it says all one needs to say about the young Juliet Crawley that I have never been more confident that we had found the right person for the job. She did not let us down, she relished frontier life and felt entirely at home taking on local customs. So, she totalled more Suzuki 4x4s on the dusty roads of the North-West Frontier than any other employee; in the overall scheme of things, it was worth it – after all, standards had to be maintained!

PESHAWAR

PESHAWAR

Making Sense out of Babel
Anthony Fitzherbert

In the late 1980s, Anthony worked for the UN Food and Agriculture Organisation, assessing the damage of Afghanistan's conflict, and then setting up and managing its agricultural rehabilitation programme. He now works as a freelance consultant on agriculture in the Near East and Central Asia.

Ten years of devastating conflict, the result of the communist coups d'état and the Soviet occupation of Afghanistan in 1978/79 brought about the destruction of that unfortunate country's society and body-politic, laid waste its infrastructure, destroyed its economy and its rural villages at unbelievable cost in human life and livelihood. The consequences of those years are still with us.

By the late 1970s, Peshawar, the previously well-ordered capital of British India's North-West Frontier Province, situated at the bottom of the famous Khyber Pass, had become somewhat faded and run-down since the partition of India and the formation of independent Pakistan in 1947. Then, in the 1980s, Peshawar acquired a new life and a new character, when as a consequence of this last bloody paroxysm of the Cold War that raged across the plains and mountains of Afghanistan, the town became the wild-east capital of the frontier of Central Asia. Some five million Afghan refugees, of diverse ethnic and sectarian origin, fled to Pakistan escaping conflict and the destruction of their villages. A cross-section and almost a third of that country's population were now living in tented, foetid refugee camps strung out along the frontier.

Peshawar become a chaotic boom town on the back of a gold-rush of aid, arms and opium, in which an astonishing diversity of humanity from a score of different nations were brought together and rubbed shoulders. Bearded, turbaned tribesmen wearing their *patou* shawls like the togas of Roman senators, with their *burqa*-shrouded women and grubby-faced children, already learning to play cricket in the camps. Peshawar had become a city of spies, spooks, crooks, cranks and Cold War warriors; dealers in arms, opium and snake oil remedies; aid workers, young and old, male and female, the saintly and the sinful, the brave and the craven. Heroic frontline medics, war correspondents full of derring-do; journalists, both the honest and the dishonest, the drunk and the

Fynn on his third birthday with his new present, a donkey cart

sober; Pakistani soldiers, policemen and *khasadars*, peasants, bureaucrats, politicians and political agents; United Nations officials of all hues and homelands, efficient and inefficient, the selfless and dedicated as well as the self-serving.

The centre of social activity for this frontier tower of Babel was the bar of the American Club where throats dry with Afghan dust could be slaked and tall tales told of adventures in the Panjshir and the Paktia valleys. Where light entertainment was provided to weary cold-warriors and humanitarians alike, by the Burl Ives figure of its self-appointed barman and campaign cartoonist, Steve Masty. Steve with his guitar and his satirical 'Country and Eastern' lyrics from which neither mujahideen commanders, humanitarian aid agencies, the United Nations, nor the inhabitants, customs, climate and food of the Punjab escaped.

It was into this world that Juliet Crawley, together with an eccentric, talented, musical linguist, Bruce Wannell, came in 1986 to manage the newly formed British aid agency known as Afghanaid. An NGO, initially founded more as a support arm for the mujahideen military *jihad* against the occupying Soviets and the supposedly Communist Afghan government of Dr Najibullah, than the more staid and respectable aid and development agency the organisation later became and still is. Driving ambulances, delivering medicines and other things to the hard-pressed 'fighters for the faith', they picked up the wounded, and even sent some to Britain for special medical treatment, where they were lodged with Juliet's friends and relations. This was about the time the Americans finally agreed to give the mujahideen the Stinger ground-to-air missile that tipped the balance of conflict in their favour as the economy and resolve of the USSR began to crumble.

Juliet was a prime candidate to find herself the wife of the heir to some ancient name and country estate. Châtelaine of some fine old Queen Anne or Georgian manor house, pillar of the community and the church, guardian of a beautiful garden, surrounded by children, dogs and horses. Peshawar saw to it that this was not to be quite like that.

She was already a widow when I first met her in 1988 or 1989, I forget which. Her first husband, Dominque Vergos, a French photo-journalist specialising in human tragedy and conflict, had been murdered in mysterious circumstances one winter's night as he went out to feed the dogs in the compound of their house in Peshawar. Contrary to expectations and despite the violent tragedy of her husband's death, Juliet remained in Peshawar, arraying herself fetchingly in widow's weeds of black. She continued to face life with a boldness and beauty that earned her the sobriquet, among the aid community, of the Black Widow. Her small son, Fynn, being gently cared for, not by a comfortable round *ayah*, but by a bearded, be-turbaned Afghan warrior, grew up in the company of a menagerie of animals and birds that filled their compound. This included a

Fynn and Juliet with a donkey, part of the menagerie in Peshawar

camel, a horse and a donkey, several *kuchi* shepherd dogs and a small flock of pinioned cranes!

By this time Juliet had left her work with Afghanaid, its buccaneering days over. It was now busily turning itself into a more conventional aid and development agency. She was now working under a United Nations contract commissioned to supervise the completion of a series of socio-economic studies of the various Afghan provinces and districts across the frontier from Pakistan. This was work that particularly suited her talents and for which she engaged the help of a very effective network of aid agency workers, with a bent for intelligence gathering, and other friends, *faranghi* as well as Afghan, that included Scandinavians as well as the French 'pied noir' inhabitants of the notorious 'Maison Blanche'. I still have a set of these studies in my Afghan archives. They have never been bettered.

It was not until about 1999 or 2000 that I met Juliet again when visiting friends and relations in Yorkshire. Having been widowed twice in violent circumstances, she was by now living near her sister, Priscilla. She had also lost her eye to cancer and was now wearing a black patch, which she did with the same panache as she had worn her widow's weeds in Peshawar.

She was now immersing herself in local Tadcaster affairs, riding to hounds with the Middleton and York & Ainsty and devoting her energies to the formation of the Rory Peck Trust. Every Christmas a card would arrive from Juliet. Not of cosy nativity scenes, but usually a photograph of one or other of her children, gun in hand with a rabbit or pigeon they had slain.

My working connection with Afghanistan continued periodically throughout the 1990s and I returned more intensely in late 2001 and 2002 and thereafter, when among other things I led a wild-life expedition into the Wakhan and the Pamirs in September/October 2002. Nothing daunted, a year or two later Juliet, with friends, herself set off to trek into the Wakhan and the Afghan Pamir so I was able to tell her something of what she was likely to find there. Later I heard a rumour that they had been arrested by a patrol of the Chitral Scouts when they crossed the Boroghil pass into Chitral. Of course Juliet had friends in Chitral as well, in the shape of the Ul Mulk family, and that lovely old warrior Colonel Kush, then still living in his mud fortress of Mastuj, who was able to bail them out. I think that must have been almost her last great adventure on the 'Frontier' that she enjoyed so much.

No Austen Lady

Alastair Crooke

After leaving MI6, Alastair set up Conflicts Forum, an organisation based in Beirut that promotes engagement between Islam and the West. His articles about the Middle East and Islamist movements appear frequently in the international press.

Sitting down to write about Juliet evokes many thoughts. Naturally, many are about her, but also, many are about a particular age: the era of Peshawar of the eighties – of Afghanistan as it was then, of Islam then, of her as a woman in that Islamic world of the mujahideen. And recalling it in this way fills me with a sense of seasons long gone. As I try to envision it, it feels as if I am picking through those old black-and-white photographs that seem drawn from a different world: of Beirut of the bustling thirties – so different to post-civil war, cold, 'reproduction' downtown that has somehow lost all human vibrancy and intimacy.

What do I mean? Juliet was no Jane Austen-esque young woman absorbed with her own tender, and very vulnerable sensibilities. She was quite a tomboy. But also at ease with being feminine – and with *who she was*. There was none of this contemporary compulsive scratching away at her 'identity'; none of the identity 'confusion', or today's narcissistic self-voyeurism. She was courageous, surely, throughout her life, but never made a point of it. It was not important. In fact, with most of what she did, she simply 'got on with it', never stopping to consider if she should somehow 'showcase' her courage or her selflessness for 'career reasons'. Nothing would be less in character for her. Her courage, her immediate active impulse, on facing human misfortune, was entirely without any affectation. How different that is to today. Perhaps we forget how much, and how quickly, the ethos of an age changes?

At that time, Juliet used to engage – perhaps I should say that she would 'glide' – effortlessly into familiarity with the Islamist Afghan resistance leaders. Again, it was never an issue. They took her 'as she was', and treated her as an honorary man. Neither party seemed troubled by this pragmatic arrangement. Neither seemed belittled by it. The meetings were always humorous and laced with wry jests and smiles.

Afghanistan. Juliet with one of the leading figures of Takhar in around 1986. History relates that he asked Juliet to marry him

But as I recall this, it also makes me think how unlikely such an occurrence would be today. Sunni Islam has changed as much as has downtown Beirut. It is not what it was. It seems now an age past: but then Sunni Islam was laced with worthy portions of wisdom, knowledge of the world's foibles, and above all warmth. What happened? There has been crisis: huge turmoil, and the 'cultural revolution' of intolerant, puritan Wahhabism.

And of Afghanaid? It did simple things, like help people – people who were in need of assistance. Looking back, it was somehow much less *ideological* than today's NGO equivalents. I do not recall that Afghanaid had a *mission statement*, or an empirical system of measurement for Juliet's 'performance quotients'. It did not, as far as I recall, have an intent to 'liberate' Afghan women, or instil democracy, or even teach human rights. It occupied itself, I think, with matters more basic: getting medical assistance to those who were injured, and helping those who had lost a leg (on the innumerable, undetectable mines), to learn to walk again with an artificial leg.

Juliet with the Big Man of Takhar again, in 2004

So, are such musings mere nostalgia for something long gone? Well, in one sense, perhaps yes. It reminds us how much has changed: how much *we* have changed, since Juliet lived in Peshawar. But it is *not* maudlin. It is something genuinely lost.

99

Juliet's 'naïveté' – if that is how it would be seen in today's commercialised world – comprised a certain 'integrity' that is viewed as *passé* today. If she were to know now, as we do today, that the US had deliberately fired up an Islamist rebellion in Afghanistan, months before the Soviet invasion, precisely in order to provoke a Soviet occupation, and led Russia into a debilitating, and bloody quagmire (as Zbigniew Brzezinski, President Carter's National Security Advisor, now proudly admits), would she have baulked at it? Would she have thought that bloodying Russia's nose, in revenge for America's defeat in Vietnam, was worth all the spilled blood?

Ours, of course, is now a more cynical age; but would that understanding – if known then – have deterred Juliet? We cannot tell for sure, but I guess that it would not. I think her integrity was directed more towards the individual human condition than it was shaped by the cynical calculus of power and geo-politics.

Immediately!
Richard Cleghorn Brown

Richard was running a project to develop portable satellite transmitters for reporting the Afghan–Soviet war. His team could be credited to be the creators of a medium that has come to dominate news-gathering.

If someone had told her that she epitomised a veritable modern-age saint, Juliet would have exploded in a convulsive guffaw: she would be the last to consider herself in such an august role. But, due to her gentle consideration for others and resolved persistence, she well-nigh deserved such an accolade. For Juliet would enable results which the recipient would never cease to be grateful for, or truly forget for the rest of their life.

A lot of these things were not just in formal, structured activities, such as when she was working in a leper colony in southern India or as an assistant field officer with Afghanaid in Peshawar; she also undertook extra, voluntary work. She didn't have to, but she realised that there was something that ought to be done – and did it because, otherwise, it would probably never be done by anyone else.

Juliet pushed her care for humanity way beyond the norm. Her own dogged example achieved admiration and respect. *She* would instigate, whilst others sat on their hands. *She* would find what needed to be done, and, if no one came forward, she would do it herself. This could be unnerving sometimes: she would acquire additional help without waiting for nominal permissions. When mujahideen needed treatment, Juliet would find people to look after them in London, whether or not they were 'approved' by the authorities. She would say, 'Why not?' For, otherwise, an increasing inventory would have had to accumulate back in Peshawar until eventually they *just might* have been lucky enough to have come to the front of a list … if they were still alive. Juliet realised things were that critical.

No matter how deeply involved she had become in a particular project, Juliet was never too busy to listen to other people's pressing considerations. She would always do what she could – and would do it *immediately*! To make time for all this was astonishing. Yet Juliet would, time and time again, and virtually alone, come up with the goods as and when they were really needed.

During the days of 'Satellite House', things became even more complicated in Peshawar. But, for these convolutions, Juliet just became even more valuable. Over several years, there were some fifteen to twenty people living regularly at the house. Vehicles came and went. Mysterious objects were delivered. Things were taken in and out for trials and evaluation. Electrical generators went away and were brought back. Shiny devices with wires were brought in and out …

As operations moved towards their final conclusions, it became more and more critical that there should be no dislocation to the activities at the house. But it would be only a matter of time before people began to add things up. The owner of Satellite House was a powerful Shinwari tribal leader, who lived at the far end of the Khyber Pass at Landi Kotal. If this man were to become alarmed at what was going on, it could have spelt the end for the entire satellite project. So, on his occasional visits into Peshawar, it became essential that someone was instantly available to reassure the Shinwari that everything was being well taken care of, and that there was *nothing ostensibly remarkable* at all about anything being undertaken there. They would have to keep the tribal leader so happy with reassurances of his monthly tranches of cash that he would not want to pry at all into the precise nature of the equipment and activities there or actually see the two revolutionary mobile satellite uplink transmitters under preparation for deployment into Afghanistan. All this they would have to do without the tribal leader going into the house itself.

Needless to say, Juliet was not the slightest bit fased at the prospect of being asked to fend off the tribal leader's detailed questions. Although not familiar with the technology itself, she would merely deflect matters into more mundane monetary spheres. Moreover, when the tribal leader posited that Satellite House should be totally refurbished by the project at its end at a ridiculously exaggerated expense, Juliet's clear and firm, but polite, disagreements to his proposal saved the day. Indeed, everyone actually went away happy – what an achievement, and yet another feather in her capable cap. If anybody could deal with a fiery furnace, Juliet could.

Juliet somehow always seemed to strike exactly the right thing to do. To take a lighter-hearted example, consider 'Hook', 'Line' and 'Sinker' (or 'Shadrach', 'Meshach' and 'Abednego') – the three pet cranes who lived in the Satellite House compound. With her generous consideration for even animals, Juliet would zealously ensure that no harm was done to even those species, in spite of the fact that the *chowkidar*s and visiting Afghans were apt to try to use such birds as target-practice for their AK-47s. No. Horses and dogs should also be respected! So assiduous was she that, on at least two occasions when visiting the Afghanaid house, people were surprised to find scrawny Tonga ponies contentedly munching the *mali*'s carefully tended garden plants. Juliet had rescued the emaciated and abused creatures in the bazaar by simply buying the ponies outright from the bemused *tonga-wallah*s.

Juliet would always know what needed to be done. And do it! Immediately!

Humour through Tragedy
Robert Salisbury

Robert helped establish the Afghan Support Committee and Afghanaid, organisations which were set up in the early eighties in response to the 1979 coup in Afghanistan and the subsequent Soviet intervention.

Juliet Peck took a dim view of feebleness. Her own opinions were robust and forcibly and economically expressed. To suggest support for the European Union, banning hunting or teetotalism would attract a snort of derision followed by a collapse into uncontrollable giggles. She had an unerring eye for the absurd. It was perhaps a quality that helped sustain her extraordinary resilience.

It was a resilience she would be forced to draw on to a degree few are called upon to match. Both her husbands were shot, one in Peshawar and one in Moscow, and she herself fought a battle against various forms of cancer over many years. It was a battle which did not inhibit her from pursuing whatever project was for the time being occupying her mind.

Not long before she died, I had an exchange with Juliet which in retrospect seems wholly characteristic.

'You said you would like me to come with you to Central Asia.' (There were usually few preliminaries in telephone conversations with Juliet.)

'Well, I would, but you said you might be dead by April which is when I am going, so I thought you might be otherwise engaged.'

'Well, I am not going to be dead and of course I'm coming.' And, of course, she did. She was dying, but it was not going to stop her.

Her experience in what was then called the North-West Frontier Province of Pakistan showed to great advantage on that trip. She engaged with the locals who seemed to take her directness in their stride. In an interview with one official in Uzbekistan about the heroin trade, she cut through my rather mealy-mouthed approach and gave him a *mauvais quart d'heure* which was illuminating to her companions and which he did not seem to resent.

I first met Juliet in the early 1980s when she came to work in the London office of the Afghan Support Committee and its sister group Afghanaid. Juliet ran the office with the help of a bossy fox terrier. Both had only recently come down from Edinburgh University and Juliet's principal objective was to get herself transferred to our office in Peshawar where she could exercise her penchant for action and skulduggery.

There were obvious impediments to her going. She had no experience of the area or particular knowledge of Islamic societies. Peshawar was not wholly safe and we were very much trying to learn the ropes ourselves. Our resistance needless to say crumbled and I found myself feebly trying to reassure her parents that she would be fine and that, anyway, if we did not send her, she would find some other way of going which might be riskier.

In Peshawar, she rapidly established herself, with few resources at her disposal, as an effective planner of aid programmes and as a good judge both of local personalities and of what was happening in Afghanistan and Pakistan. Although she had an unerring ear for the bogus, she did possess a romantic streak and she was not immune to the romance of the Frontier and the story of the Great Game under the Raj. This gave her a sympathy for local people and traditions which helped make her effective. She was far from being the 'rather Sloaney girl' that one senior visiting British official described her as when he returned to London after a visit to Peshawar.

This romantic streak may have made her first husband irresistible to her. Dominique Vergos was a handsome, tough Frenchman who had spent years in Afghanistan in the 1970s. He was one of a number of his compatriots who had become expert in Afghan matters and who at that time made important contributions to the understanding of what was going on. He had returned to Peshawar from Afghanistan with a collection of pictures which showed a photographer of genius.

It took no time at all for them to marry. Their son Fynn is the remarkable product of their union. I have often wondered

Juliet and Dominique in Lahore, 1987

how their lives would have developed had Dominique not been assassinated one Christmas in the garden of their house in Peshawar. Juliet's calm in the face of tragedy when she rang to report what had happened made the deepest impression on me.

Her husband's murder seemed to make no difference to her determination to continue working in Peshawar, where she stayed until the Soviets left Afghanistan. By that time she had married again, this time to Rory Peck, an Irish freelance cameraman who had for some time been active in filming the Afghan–Soviet war. He was brave to the point of foolhardiness and the pictures he took were as a result hyper-realistic.

Both Juliet and Rory felt the action was moving elsewhere and the news would be made in Moscow, where there were clearly opportunities for freelancers. Undeterred, as always, by their chronic shortage of money, and the now imminent arrival of Lettice, they set off and established themselves at the centre of events as the Soviet empire entered its death throes, throes accelerated by the events in Afghanistan they had themselves in a small way encouraged.

Rory's style of reporting did not change. His every instinct was to film as close to the action as he could. It is hardly surprising that he found himself in the White House filming the resistance to the attempted counter-revolution and in the line of fire. So Juliet lost her second husband. By this time she was suffering from her first tumour and she lost an eye as a result.

I met her shortly after Rory's death by sheer chance at Sheremetyevo airport as she left for England. She was travelling with both her children, piles of luggage, an eye patch, a merry look in her eye and an indomitable spirit. I felt like weeping for an England which seemed to have passed for everyone except her.

She returned to a farmhouse in Yorkshire whose grounds she immediately declared an EU-free zone. She hunted ferociously on an immense one-eyed horse and, in fits of giggles, delivered herself of devastating *obiter dicta* on the foibles of the more absurd people of her acquaintance and on the cowardice of civil servants and their political masters.

She devoted much effort to establishing the Rory Peck Trust in memory of her second husband. It flourishes and supports and trains freelancers and their families all over the world. Its annual award ceremony is the highlight of the freelancers' year and its awards are universally coveted. It stands as much as a memorial to Juliet as to Rory.

She commanded the unswerving loyalty of her friends. Her courage and fortitude were astonishing; her jokes and joy in life a happy memory for all who knew her.

Lapsang and Stallions
Kim Keating

Kim worked for Afghanaid while her husband, Michael, was the Peshawar representative of 'Operation Salaam', the initiative to help reconstruct Afghanistan. What follows describes the moment when Kim first met Juliet, in 1989.

Tea at Juliet's bungalow was served in the garden, an immaculately chipped Russian Gardner tea set brought out on a tray into the grassless, dusty compound. We sat in worn armchairs beneath the mulberry trees that generated both a much-needed roof of shade above and a sticky red carpet of crushed fruit below. The end-of-day heat was intense, the call to prayer from the next-door mosque put small talk on hold, and the bulbuls darted around.

We sipped our Lapsang tea and nibbled the dry bazaar-bought biscuits. Juliet's dogs lolled about, a

Juliet in the summer of 1986

small terrier, a pointer straight out of *Horse & Hound* and a third wolf-like beast with no ears, as befits an Afghan *kuchi* cur. Juliet told me that Dominique had driven it as a puppy across northern Afghanistan in a motorbike saddlebag to give to her. The dog, very much not a puppy any more with its steely blue eyes, intense and unremitting stare, intimidating fangs and enormous bulk, crouched inches from my plate of biscuits. It did not, like much in Juliet's orbit, make me relax.

Juliet sat upright in full riding kit, serious knee-length lace-up leather boots more suited to a nineteenth-century Indian mess, khaki jodhpurs and immaculately starched shirt buttoned to her neck, a huge belt around her tiny waist. In her hand she held a cat-o'nine-tails with which she swotted the *kuchi* dog. It felt good that she was on my side; I hoped it would stay that way.

'Which stallion do you want?' she asked, passing me another tasteless biscuit. 'They all bite and fight each other.' It was then that I noticed the horses in the shaded corners of her tiny compound, each just out of kicking range of its neighbour. None would have been welcome at a Home Counties gymkhana club. They were sinewy, barely broken, ears plastered flat back, eyes wild, mad with anger, ready to assault anyone or anything who came within kicking distance. Each was already covered with a film of sweat, white foam pouring down their back legs and shoulders as they lunged and tore at their tethers.

'They're keen to get out for a ride,' Juliet pronounced cheerfully. I tried to imagine how the young *chowkidar* had saddled the animals – and survived. 'I'm not as good a rider as Kim,' said Michael, bravely suppressing his nervousness. 'Then you'd better not fall off'. 'This,' she added, brandishing her cat-o'nine-tails, 'is for the people who get in our way. Follow me.'

Minutes later we grabbed flying manes, reins, anything that seemed vaguely solid, and charged out the gates into the cooling, suddenly rural evening air, dust and hooves flying, horses lurching and screaming behind Juliet's slight frame, her long hair unashamedly exposed, effortlessly clutching her stallion in one hand and brandishing the whip in the other.

Later that evening we sat in the evening's cooling shadows, once again beneath the mulberry trees, all of us sweaty and dusty, laughing as we clutched huge gin and tonics, marvelling at the availability of the ice in this forty-five-degree climate – thanks to Juliet's diesel generator which kicked in when the daily power cut began – and the gin courtesy of the booze stocks of UNMOGIP's peacekeeping mission to Jammu and Kashmir. No mention of the obstacles overcome – stone-throwing children, bicyclists, *karezes*, goats, crazed mutts.

Baby Fynn crawled beneath our feet grabbing fearlessly at the *kuchi* hound's nose, the dog studiously unimpressed. 'Oh Fynnie, *do* grow up,' Juliet said as the toddler collided with the table and started to cry. 'You managed to stay on, Michael. Well done.' We had passed. 'More ice?'

Difficulties with Dominique
Mary and Simon Crawley

Mary and Simon are Juliet's parents.

MARY:
When Fynn was born in Peshawar, Julie was very keen that I saw him. The little chap was a very, very important person to her. I think I only met Dominique on this trip. He was there a lot then, and was always polite, gracious, accommodating, and helpful. He was very strong and wanted his way, but I think that that sort of character was what Julie liked. It was the excitement.

The second time I went to Peshawar was after Dominique was killed. The chap who had shot Dominique escaped back into Afghanistan. But his family took responsibility and this *jirga* was arranged. They had it on the veranda at her house. There are three options: you either killed the man who has killed – an eye for an eye, a tooth for a tooth; they had to pay a fine, which was a lot of money; or there was total forgiveness. Anyway, she went for the money. I never knew how much. Directly after they had handed it over, she gave it straight back to them. She knew that she wasn't going to take their money.

When it was decided, they killed a goat and made stew. That is the way in sacramental theology. The meal, a common peace offering in religions, consolidates the agreement. So that she was in it too, Julie had to eat some of this meat out of

113

the pot. Custom was satisfied and that settled it. There was no further trouble.

SIMON:

I never met Dominique, but he did come to England. He rang Patterdale to talk to Julie. She wasn't in, and had only just told me that she wanted to marry Dominique. I said to him over the telephone that I was not best pleased about this, and asked him to come to see me. When Julie came back late in the evening, I asked what it was all about – because we had heard that there was this fellow Dominique around, but it was a complete shock to me that she wanted to marry him. I said to Julie, you will do what you will do, regardless of what I say, but as your father I cannot possibly encourage a relationship with a man who has already made two women deeply unhappy and maybe many more. She went down to London to meet Dominique. I knew that if she was going to get married, she was going to have to register the marriage with the British Consul. So we sent a telegram saying 'Congratulations and best wishes from all the family'.

Then I wrote a letter to Dominique saying that, 'Although I haven't consented to this marriage I accept it as a fact and we will do everything we can to help you, and I hope that in time we shall be great friends.' Dominique never acknowledged it, and I didn't hear from him. I had rejected him, and we hadn't got to the point where we could begin to build up any kind of relationship. You must accept what is done and try and make as much good out of it as you can. I think that is the only way to cope with it.

Our relationship to her was very different from that of a friend. Sometimes, she did things which were very difficult for us not just to accept, but appreciate why she did it. Why did she marry Dominique, knowing what his background was, what he was like? It is a dreadful thing to think of Fynn's father like that, but I don't think anybody would want their daughter to marry somebody with his background. You just wouldn't. So her decisions were very complex for us. But then when she is your daughter, you want to support her, and after they married, we did. But it was a difficult time.

Within a year he was dead. He was buried in the family area of his village church near Brest.

Two Letters
Bruce Wannell

Bruce went to Peshawar in 1985 to work as field representative of Afghanaid. He is a linguist and has travelled all over the Middle East, Iran and Afghanistan.

THURSDAY, 30 DECEMBER 2010

Written after our dinner at my home at 46, Holgate Road, York

Dear Fynn,

It was a pleasure to see you and your sister this evening. As we discussed, I will here note down my memories of your father Dominique Vergos and the circumstances of his death in Peshawar, Pakistan.

Afghanaid was very short of money and in order to help with domestic expenses, rooms were let out to visiting journalists. Robert Cranborne of the Afghanaid committee in London was sending out the newly invented transmitting equipment for testing to get news rapidly from the field to broadcasters. Among other journalist guests – Peter Jouvenal, Julian Gearing – we also hosted your future step-father Rory Peck. There was no office vehicle then, so I hired two brothers, Saber and Naser of the Tsuluzai clan of Kama, Ningrahar, Afghanistan to bring their rickshaws every morning to transport anyone who needed their services.

When Juliet (then Crawley) came out to help me after one of my bouts of amoebic dysentery and jaundice, Naser and Saber were promoted to drive the office vehicles which by that time had been purchased. They quickly became devoted to your mother, whose generosity and dignity won their respect. These Pushtuns were members of the Hizb-e Islami party of Gulbuddin Hekmatyar, and had strong rivalry with the Panjshiri Tajiks who also helped run the office, who belonged to the Jami'at-e Islami party of Burhaneddin Rabbani. Juliet was ambitious and quickly wanted to run the office in her own way and preserve her own independence, though she was not so good at balancing ethnic and political rivalries within the office. Our committee in London was divided between liberal aid worker types (Elisabeth Winter) and more hawkish elements (Romey Fullerton), so we often received marching orders that were quite contradictory.

During the course of my second trip into Afghanistan, this time with the mujahideen of the Mahaz Melli party of Pir Gailani, to the base of Amin Wardak in Wardak, in 1986, I met your father who was travelling west towards Qandahar to see Mullah Madat, a tall, handsome and charismatic teacher who was the original founder of the Taleban. Dominique was travelling independently and taught me how to assess a mujahideen camp – cleanliness, order, efficiency etc. He told me of the longer periods he had spent observing such places as the Russian airbase at Shindand in the west of the country. He also told me that if he worked for three months, he expected to be able to play for the remaining nine months! I invited him to come and stay at Afghanaid when we both returned to Peshawar. I believe this was how he met your mother. Dominique had been a fashion photographer and was a dashing figure whose raffishness – and especially whose demanding taste in what an elegant woman should be – soon had a profound effect on Juliet.

After their marriage and honeymoon in the Maldives, they rented a house with a garden in University Town, not far from the American Club. Soon it filled up with a large cage of green parakeets on the back terrace, a small camel, and a *kuchi* dog with a cropped tail, which you played with as a child. Your father started working at the Swedish Committee for Afghanistan, under the liberal ex-journalist Anders Faenge, where he was commissioned to build up a database on military resistance commanders in Afghanistan, and was increasingly critical of the behaviour of Gulbuddin Hekmatyar's Hezb-e Islami. At the same time he was increasingly frustrated and often became drunk at the American Club, which led to fights with your mother, with bruises for her and scratches for him, and frequent bursts of Kalashnikov gunfire in the yard to let off steam at night. The local gossip, which had connected Dominique originally with the CIA, now concentrated on how long this situation could go on, and my Pushtun friends, the brothers Naser and Saber, expressed serious concern for your mother's safety.

I had meanwhile left Afghanaid after less than two years, had travelled independently across Afghanistan on horseback in the summer of 1987, and returned to Peshawar to select and train a team of Afghan monitors for the American medical NGO 'Freedom Medicine'. I was living down the railway

Dominique and Nathalie Vergos, France 1970

line in an enclosed courtyard house in an area not yet lived in by Europeans. Shortly afterwards, I had to go and stay with a Pakistani general, Jehanzeb Afridi, when my life and that of my servants was threatened by Hezb-e Islami after I had publicly criticised their robbery of one of our medical supply caravans destined for Shi'i Hazaras.

On the evening of your father's death, I had had some Shinwari musicians from the east of Afghanistan perform in my guest room, and we had just finished and gone to bed when at about two a.m. there was banging at the gates, and Naser was let in, shouting that 'That fool Dominique has gone and killed himself' and insisting that I come immediately. We drove to University Town and I found your mother sobbing uncontrollably over the corpse of her husband, which had been lifted on to the charpoy in the *chowkidar*'s room at the back of the garage. She managed to tell me that the body had been slumped across the door and that she had had to push with all her strength to force her way in after she heard shots fired and Dominique did not come back after one of their rows: she had been reading her Old Testament in bed to calm down. She was in such a state – great gut-wrenching groans and sobs; I was worried and went to fetch the Catholic priest to calm her. Later she told me that that night she had had a miscarriage as a result.

By the time we came back, Dr Philippe Truze, who worked with a medical NGO, had also arrived. He very calmly and efficiently pointed out the clean bullet-hole at the base of your father's skull and the smashed bone of the forehead where the bullet had emerged, and said that it was impossible that Dominique had killed himself. Rigor mortis had begun to set in, if I remember rightly – the body was difficult to move. The Pakistan police then arrived, loudly proclaiming that it was a clear case of suicide. We then looked more carefully at the wall of the *chowkidar*'s room and found brain and bone matter splattered over and above the door – your father was tall and had almost certainly been held against the door, face to the door, after some struggle, and shot by whoever had overpowered him. I found a lot of fresh cracked paint fragments on the flowers growing outside below the one small window of the *chowkidar*'s room, which was almost certainly the only way the murderers could have got out. And murderers – plural – because one man could almost certainly not have overpowered your father, even drunk – and certainly not Naser's weedy young nephew who had recently started as the night *chowkidar*, and who was later conveniently blamed for the murder.

We carried on searching and found fresh bullet-holes in the brickwork at the far end of the garage yard, in a straight line from the *chowkidar*'s room, through the garage itself where an older brown jeep was parked – its lower mudguards had also been recently perforated and another car parked in the drive: it seems that a shot or two was fired from the *chowkidar*'s room to entice your father into the room where he was killed – he was not a man to run from gunshots, especially when angry.

The American Consulate insisted on hosting the memorial service for Dominique in their garden, though he had never officially or publicly worked for them; Juliet asked me to choose texts and music for the occasion. It may, possibly, have been out of respect and affection for your mother that the Americans made this gesture; she was herself, perhaps, by that time already working for them.

Some time later, Commander Abdul Haq brokered a reconciliation between your mother and the family of the young *chowkidar* accused of the murder – it was necessary to reach some face-saving conclusion if she wanted to continue living and working in Peshawar. A *jirga* was held and a sheep sacrificed. I'm not sure if blood money was paid (probably not – your mother grandly forgave the young man, who was very probably innocent of the actual murder, though may well have been intimidated into covering for the murderers, or letting them into his room) but she settled down to life as a young widow in the same house.

The rumour of suicide was still circulating, as was another, more vicious rumour that Juliet had killed her husband herself – both absurd and patently untrue. Dr Truze's examination of the corpse also put paid to the rumour that the young *chowkidar*, panicked by Dominique's aggressive behaviour when drunk, had fired in self-defence – that would have led to bullet-wounds in the front, not the back of the head.

My interpretation takes into account the context of other incidents and murders that happened at this time of critics of Hezb-e Islami – for instance, that of Professor Sayyed Bahauddin Majruh, who wrote newsletters critical of Hezb-e Islami and was murdered at the door of his house-cum-office; or of Andy Skrypsowiak, who was murdered in Nuristan en route to visit Ahmad Shah Massoud, Gulbuddin Hekmatyar's one-time colleague and now inveterate rival (the murderers were rewarded by Hezb-e Islami with fast cars that they drove with impunity around Peshawar). My close friend Wahid of Tagao, who ran the best martial arts club in Peshawar and was a quite remarkable karate and tai-chi practitioner, was repeatedly subjected to pressure to carry out assassinations for Hezb-e Islami. He assured me that no murder was carried out unless previously vetted and passed by the Pakistani ISI – he claimed that he managed diplomatically to resist such pressure – but many may well have taken the reward and trusted the unofficial cloak of protection and secrecy.

My interpretation is that Dominique's new work for the Swedish Committee (left-liberal in its Western staff, but among its Afghan staff penetrated by Hezb-e Islami spies as well as Maoists, Pushtun nationalists etc.) certainly irritated and alarmed the Hezb-e Islami, who were the favoured party of the Pakistani

ISI and of the American CIA. The funding and overall direction may have come from that source at the top, but delegation down to grass-roots, plus ruthless manipulation by Gulbuddin with his well-honed terrorist instincts and training, meant that Hezb-e Islami was virtually unchallenged on the ground. The Americans did not want to see this reality. When Alastair Crooke sent a confidential report to the London FCO criticising the CIA's over-reliance on Hezb-e Islami, he was summoned to explain himself not to London but to Washington: not long after he left the service. I remember interpreting for Hugh Leach's confidential FCO research on Islamist movements world-wide during his Pakistan tour, and the unpleasantness of sitting so close to Gulbuddin, a really chilling monster. The decision to murder your father probably had the tacit approval, or assurance of indifference, of the Americans, who apparently had stopped employing Dominique, and probably disapproved of his extensive knowledge of Afghan commanders and Hezb-e Islami's appalling record of betrayal and murder being put on the database of a neutral and potentially critical organisation such as the Swedish Committee for Afghanistan. This may have been an added cause of his increasing frustration and turning to drink and domestic violence. The Pakistani ISI almost certainly allowed the murder, hence the pre-arranged propaganda that it was suicide: Naser, the police and the subsequent rumours all point in that

Dominique in Paris 1973–4. The photo he gave Nathalie for her bedroom wall when she went to live with her grandparents

direction. It must have been more or less facilitated by Naser and his nephew, probably out of their genuine worry about your mother's safety, and out of obedience to the party's orders. At the very least, they conveniently got out of the way while the murder was perpetrated, and Naser came to fetch me with the pre-arranged story of suicide. Not very long after, he had a serious nervous breakdown and his nerves never recovered even after he emigrated to Sweden. The fact that the young *chowkidar* did not run away – he could easily have gone back to his home area of Kama just over the border near Jalalabad – indicates that he had been given assurances of protection if he took the blame.

My dear Fynn, I hope this can help clarify what remains a murky story, and allow you to come to some sort of closure with the loss of your father when you were so young. I have not referred to diaries of the time, only to what I remember: some images are very vivid, others blurred; I have tried to indicate which, and also to separate presentation of facts from rumours heard and interpretations constructed.

With love and best wishes for 2011
Bruce Wannell

TUESDAY, 26 JANUARY 2016

Written in York after your phone call from military duty in Northern Ireland

Dear Fynn,

Once again you have asked me to write about your family, this time about your mother, whose memory remains vivid, though the memories float like disconnected images as the strict framework of time past grows vaguer.

I first met your mother in 1986 when reporting back from Peshawar to the offices of Afghanaid on an upper floor of a building in Cecil Court, London. She was sitting at a desk near the door, the first person encountered on entering the office; under the desk lurked her diminutive terrier, Thatcher. Juliet was relaxed and humorous, dressed in camel-brown colours – I remember her laughter which she often used to disarm new acquaintances. She had recently come down from Edinburgh University, and had broken off a relationship with a fellow student from Devon. She was working for the steely Romey Fullerton, who had recently introduced me to Peshawar.

The Afghanaid field office in Peshawar occupied a rented villa in a garden in Gulmohar Road along the railway line. The line ran only to the Khyber Pass. Train traffic was infrequent. When your mother came out to assist me during one of my illnesses, the railway line formed the perfect exit for her large whitish-grey horse to reach the emptier sandy areas where she could gallop at will. That horse, as difficult and temperamental as the men your mother liked, was the first significant purchase she made on arriving in Pakistan. The Panjshiri Tajik family who brokered the deal were soon lavishing hospitality on her, in a traditional Afghan bid to exercise influence: I had employed the brothers Hasham and Quddus as office orderlies, but soon they were answering only to Juliet, and were lording it over the Pushtun brothers Naser and Saber from Kama near Jalalabad. In the early days when Afghanaid had little money, I had employed these brothers to provide us with motor-rickshaws, our only transport. Later, when American money started rolling in, they graduated on to jeeps and Pajeros – though they occasionally were nostalgic for their rickshaws and once took me to an outlying Sufi shrine for a noisy all-night ceremony, attended by hordes of other rickshaw drivers.

Your mother was a good horsewoman, and her skill impressed the mujahideen commanders, especially those from the north of Afghanistan who would sponsor *buzkashi* games, when we were allowed to push our horses into the scrum to watch the sand-filled calf-carcass pulled by the mounted players at close quarters. Once, we met the large burly Uzbek commander Pahlawan Hafiz who challenged your mother to ride an angry horse which reared and kicked: she refused to be thrown, and Pahlawan became her devoted admirer, even allowing her to scold him for the appallingly dingy conditions in which he kept his wives, noticeably worse than his horses' stables and diet! I meanwhile had not covered myself in glory, allowing the grey to bolt with me one early morning when Juliet was unable to exercise him, and Quddus watched laughing helplessly as I whizzed by, scattering gravel and almost knocking over refugee market stalls on the outskirts of University Town.

The number of horses grew: your mother soon had five, and Peshawar's summer climate, often approaching fifty degrees Celsius and with high humidity, was not kind to them. So, one year, your mother asked me and Frederic Roussel to accompany her and her Arab groom and a stocky Panjshiri dwarf to cooler hill-country where the horses could be left for the hot season. I suggested Swiss friends who were running a forestry project in northern Swat. The horses and grooms were duly sent up and we followed a few days later. From there we rode through the largely trackless forests of Tal-Lamutai in Dir, with villagers bringing us bowls of yoghurt as we passed. Frederic shouted at the horses with such vigour and authority that my pony, distracted by some distant mare on heat, and who was totally ignoring my attempts to keep him in control, forthwith returned to obedience; your mother always looked self-possessed, sitting on the charpoy string-beds while I made conversation in Pushtu when we stayed at little forts, where the sons of our hosts gave us welcome leg-massages in the evening; and so on to the ever-hospitable anglophile Chitrali princes over the Lowari Pass, which we crossed on the day of Eid. When we reached the first of the *shahzadas*, a bottle of whisky was accepted and we were able to camp in the orchard by the river.

In Chitral town we went riding on narrow paths along the river with a handsome young French couple, at breakneck speed, then stopped to watch the polo: every goal was celebrated with a fanfare from the drums and oboe-like instruments with a piercing reedy noise. At the end, the leader of the winning team performed a slow, Pyrrhic dance as he left the polo-ground. Juliet had to get back to Peshawar by plane, Frederic was going off in another direction and I was due to take the five horses and two grooms on to the village of Pasti on the slopes of the highest mountain in Chitral, Tirich Mir. Frederic entrusted his saddlebags to Juliet to take back to Peshawar. The next we heard, she was being held in custody and questioned by airport security: Frederic had forgotten to tell her that the saddlebags contained his loaded pistol. She was holding her own when my French doctor friend arrived, telling the security officer not to be so childish: luckily the doctor played polo with the officer, so Juliet was able to board the plane – rather late – and resume her office work in Peshawar.

Your mother had never fallen into the trap of wearing cheap Pakistani *shalwar kameez*, almost the uniform of the American missionary girls and Mennonites. She remained resolutely English in her dress and manner – but she was also sensitive to the culture of the Afghans, and earned their respect by generosity, tact and trust. This sometimes seemed like bravura. Saber needed to borrow money: the family was always falling into further feuds with disaffected or disreputable cousins. Juliet gave it to him out of her own funds, never asking for any guarantee of repayment in writing or for any witness to the transaction. '*Elle avait de la classe*', as the French would say. Once your father Dominique's influence grew, she also had style – daring little black dresses worn to evening parties, with bold jewellery. From the moment she arrived in Peshawar, she made it obvious that she was not taking orders and was fully intent on following her own agenda. Once she had helped remove me from the organisation, she gave me a splendid farewell party on the lawns at Gulmohar Road, where musicians played and I danced with my anthropologist friend Benedicte and our Afghan friends praised the *kabutar-bazi*. In the end she didn't take over my job; a rather dull, but safe, character took over and bureaucracy took hold.

I stayed with an Afghan family in town, then moved into a low whitewashed courtyard hotel. Juliet and Dominique moved into a house in University Town where the deep terrace sheltered a large cage of green parakeets and a fluffy, cuddly, nomad puppy whose tail had been cropped. In the garden

Fynn with Dominique looking at the parakeets, Peshawar 1988

127

another gift from nomad mujahideen commanders, a small camel, was one of your playthings – but you have probably forgotten that. I benefited from leaving the aid agency with its school-uniform and tent-making programmes for war-wounded refugees, and went to train Afghan monitors to travel in-country to evaluate civilian aid given to communities free from Russian Communist control. Juliet worked more and more with the Americans, Dominique eventually with the Swedish Committee for Afghanistan, as a result of which he was murdered: but that I have described in my other letter to you.

***

We next met in London, when I returned from three years in Africa. She invited me to Yorkshire, where since her second bereavement and the loss of her eye to cancer, she was enjoying the hospitality of her brother-in-law in a row of cottages at Healaugh. Russell was your Welsh male nanny. He used to drive you at high speed to go shopping. When your mother travelled to London by train it was always first class, with smart fur coats – your mother loved luxury, and was very impressed by grand people, whose political opinions she adopted eagerly, pro-hunting, anti-European etcetera.

Sometimes, in spite of her self-discipline, she seemed to lose her moral compass. One admirer and lover, used for his title and his letterhead cachet, helped garner support for the Rory Peck Awards for war journalists and cameramen – until he was chewed up and spat out. When this former admirer was packing up, he told me how he had accompanied your mother to befriend the Ogoni people, struggling to preserve their tribal lands in southern Nigeria from the encroaching pollution of oil exploitation by Shell, resulting in the murder of Ken Sarawiwa. Juliet had posed as their friend, while all the time being paid by Shell. Similarly, she befriended the 'Swampy' eco-activists living up trees to delay destruction of natural habitat for motorway-building, while actually working for the motorway lobby; so also her attempt to penetrate the operations of Cable and Wireless in the Caribbean, etc., etc. Her love of luxury, mixing with grand people and of devious manipulation came at a cost – people were hurt and they spilled truths with some bitterness.

She said more than once to me that if it were not for her children she would have given up the struggle to live. Your mother enriched our lives. She was a complex, often difficult character, but stylish, admirable, fun, courageous, generous and defiant. Her memory will live into the future, with her friends, and in you her children.

With love to you and Lettice,
Bruce Wannell

A Farewell Letter

Rozy Aalam

Rozy Vojdany Aalam is presently living in Paris where she writes and is a designer in the applied arts.

Dear, dear Juliet,

When the Chinese want to wish you well, they say, 'May you not live in interesting times'. Well, my friend, we obviously didn't come across a Chinese sage, given the context in which we met and bonded.

When I first arrived in Peshawar in the stifling heat of the summer of 1989, having taken a field mission with the International Red Cross, I certainly did not expect all that ensued beyond the expected trials of humanitarian aid we were both engaged in. I, with a tightly knit Swiss organisation; you, with Afghanaid. Of course, we mostly lived and related within the confines of University Town, that 'safe haven' of NGOs harbouring among others the old-timers who had been bitten by the Afghan bug, and who had made the Afghan mujahideen's cause of liberating Afghanistan from the Soviet yoke their own. An interesting cast of characters emerged in this alien landscape. Die-hard aid workers, journalists, diplomats, spies-cum-informers of predominantly European and American nationalities, mostly with a smattering of Dari, sporting *shalwar kameez* and *pakol*s and mingling in times of leisure with compatriots and key Afghan refugees. Forays into

Afghanistan kept the adrenaline gushing. To our knowledge, none of our coterie of acquaintances were the arms dealers and drug traffickers that we knew milled about in Peshawar. It didn't stop us from conjecturing who was doing what under whichever guise. Beyond this microcosm of a community, a more exotic cast of characters influencing our daily preoccupations and conversations were, of course, the Afghan mujahideen. A few commanders garnered our sympathy and others our apprehensions and distrust. Then there were the thousands of refugees with whom we dealt professionally and, being an endearing people, sometimes personally. Oddly enough, we felt secure despite the lackadaisical *inshallah*-fuelled Pakistani drivers.

I believe I never told you the impression you made on me the day I accompanied our friend Bruce to your house for the first time. Granted, your reputation had preceded you. I knew that you had been recently widowed under tragic circumstances shrouded in mystery. Your husband whose son you bore seemed a legendary figure amongst the local population: a Frenchman cutting a dashing figure on horseback; a war photographer shooting film alongside the valiant Afghan freedom fighters in the mountains and the plains. There was a brawl and then a murder by your own *chowkidar*, a tragedy you suspected was politically motivated. You stayed in Peshawar, determined to get to the bottom of it. Don't forget, Juliet, I entered this landscape fresh after having lived in Hollywood and this was the stuff of the silver screen. I couldn't wait to meet you.

Upon entering the garden in which your house stood, a donkey milled about on the lawn, not far from a grazing goat. An adorable toddler (Fynn) was chasing chickens and in turn was being chased, entreated and cajoled by a heaving Afghan *nanneh*. Classical music and the scent of jasmine permeated the veranda where an Afghan houseboy was handling the tea tray. And there you were, a slightly built, fair-haired and peachy-skinned unassuming young woman. You were dressed in a riding habit, sitting on the edge of a massive mahogany recliner, a fan whirling overhead. You had set up a household which recalled the genteel days of the British Raj. I thought to myself, here's a haven of civilisation in this torrid, noisy, precarious chaos that is Peshawar. Your house welcomed an assortment of interesting people at all times – testimony to your hospitality and generosity of spirit. Teatime and Happy Hour were forums of vibrant conversation between relief workers, passing reporters and Afghanophiles.

Though professionally we were involved in the same cause, we were different in many ways. I think that at first you were intrigued by the diversity of my background. Being Persian yet Swiss enough to work for the ICRC; speaking Dari and relating to the Afghans with an ease that comes with cultural affinity; fluent in American English – which I am certain made you cringe at first encounter. You see, dear Juliet, you had a healthy dose of snobbism, which I suppose I may also have had. Neither one of us suffered fools and I enjoyed your particular brand of humour when it came to discriminating between whom you would mix with and whom you wouldn't. I believe that it was the feeling of empathy that played a determining role. Proud and reluctant as you were to divulge your innermost grief, you considered me a kindred soul who had also recently suffered a tragic loss.

Yes, we did live in interesting times. And they got even more interesting. A few months after we met, Saddam invaded Kuwait. An ominous uncertainty reigned in Peshawar where the Pakistanis no longer eyed us with their laidback benevolence. Our usually fawning tailor told us not to show up in the bazaar again. Rickshaw drivers ignored us when we hailed them. As Westerners, we were looked upon with disdain and suspicion. The atmosphere was incendiary, thanks in part to what blared from the minarets. All it would take was a spark and all hell would break loose. The UN and ICRC advised us not to venture beyond our homes and the headquarters. It wasn't a long stretch between where we lived and on that weekend I was due to come over to your place for tea. I was to meet Rory for the first time, so had asked the cook to bake you a cake. Rory was passing through on his way to Iraq where he, Peter Jouvenal and John Simpson were due to cover the war.

When I called you to confirm the time, you told me to rush over at once. You would explain when I got there. Ah, I thought to myself. Juliet must have some urgent news to relay to me. You might recall that my husband had been one of the four ICRC delegates in Quetta who had been taken hostage by a renegade mujahideen group a few weeks back and I had been worried sick since then. I drove in through the gate, you appeared in the garden, wearing a dress for a nice change, and frantically ushered me and the cake into a car with Bruce and Peter. Rory and little Fynn were waiting for you in the other vehicle. I didn't know what to think. Was this an escape of sorts? Where are we all going, I asked Peter. 'To church,' he said. 'Rory and I are shortly leaving for Iraq and the two of them just decided to get married before we take off!' I was to be the maid of honour, Peter was to be the best man and Bruce was going to play the wedding march on the organ. Who but you, Juliet, would get married on the spur of the moment like this?

So the cortège of two cars took off for the little church whose pastor I had once met at your house. Midway along the notorious trunk road, your car came to a standstill at a kerb. We followed suit and waited patiently behind. We could see that you and Rory were having a heated argument. Finally, Peter went over to see what the problem was. He came back grinning widely and said that we might have to turn back. 'Why?' I asked. 'They don't seem to agree on the marriage vows,' said Peter, wryly. 'Juliet refuses to say "obey" after "I promise to love, honour, and …"'

Oh Juliet, who else but you?

You seemed to have gotten your way because I didn't hear the word 'obey' in the marriage vows. I was turning pages for Bruce at the organ, and as I got it all wrong he ground his teeth. Fynn, in the guise of a little pageboy, was more interested in banging on the organ than presenting the ring at the altar. The whole episode seemed like a vaudeville act. You having not pledged to obey Rory, we traipsed off to the rectory where we had a rather sedate tea and cake with the pastor and his wife.

Rory returned from Baghdad to Peshawar within a week. It was the following day when I got a call from the ICRC hospital next door to the Delegation to inform me that you had been admitted with a broken back. And I thought you were having a honeymoon. When I rushed over to see you, you

Rory and Juliet after their wedding

were stabilised on a stretcher and already sedated. Here I was in my supposed territory, and I felt helpless to do anything for you. The least I could do was to arrange for a makeshift private room for you to have some privacy with Rory, sparing you the wards with the Afghan casualties and their families. I was petrified that with a broken back you might be paralysed, as indeed the doctors feared. When you were more alert the following day, you greeted me with your usual wry smile. 'Not much of a honeymoon, huh?' I commented. 'I didn't fall. It was the horse that slipped in the mud and threw us down.' Not that I questioned your horsemanship!

You tackled your recovery in Yorkshire with your usual determination, and true to form, surprised me with the news that you had been pregnant with Lettice all along. You were now off on another adventure with Rory in Central Asia – did we not encounter each other there?

Our paths crossed again in England at Rory's memorial service. Oh Juliet, how could you have been so tragically widowed once again? And within weeks, having to come to terms with the loss of an eye. Well … you wore the eye patch with panache and poured your energy into creating the Rory Peck Trust. In those years when we both lived in England, each with our own brand of adversity, your loyalty as a friend did not once waver. I believe that we gave each other unqualified comfort. We could let our guards down and not always have to present a brave front.

I never knew how threatening your reoccurring cancer had become. How could I, when you convinced me that you could once again beat it? I preferred to believe you than to rely on my own misgivings, having seen my husband succumb to the same cancer. I had moved to Paris by then and therefore was not witness to any decline in your condition.

The last time I saw you, you called to tell me you were coming to Paris with Fynn. I had you over for dinner and we had a jolly time. The little toddler Fynn had turned into a handsome and delightful young man. You seemed well enough but curiously not interested in seeing the latest of my jewellery creations, preferring to converse about things closer to your heart. It was only after you and Fynn had left that I realised you had come to make your adieu. We lost you, dear friend, very shortly afterwards.

Whenever I think of you, the Book of Job comes to mind – for you had far more than a fair share of adversity and heartache to overcome. You soldiered on with your signature humour and timid smile. You remain with me as an example and source of inspiration.

As always, with love,
Rozy

The French Doctor
Fiona Gall

Fiona Gall currently works in Kabul for an NGO and has been in the region – Afghanistan, Pakistan and India – since the 1980s.

B efore I first met Juliet in Peshawar, I bumped into Rory, her future husband. A girlfriend and I had travelled up to Chitral as tourists and took a local bus to visit the hot springs at Garam Chasma. This was in fact a huge arrival point for many Afghan refugees fleeing the fighting against the Russians in the 1980s and a departure point for caravans of horses and mujahideen with their equipment going back in to Afghanistan. We left the scrubby village of Garam Chasma and walked up the road towards the pass – welcomed on all sides by friendly refugee families camping on the sides of the road. In traditional fashion, they all asked us in for tea. Finally, having walked far enough, we turned round and picked one tent to stop at where there were plenty of ladies. We sat with the family for at least an hour – drinking tea and gesturing to each other with signs as we had no common language. The man of the family then came into the tent, he did speak a bit of English, and he told us that he had a French doctor staying in his second tent behind us. We were rather surprised to hear this. Our host then insisted we go next door to introduce ourselves. We found Rory, 'the French doctor', sitting in his tent reading a book and obviously annoyed to be displayed to two women tourists by his host. He explained that he was waiting to go into Afghanistan and was hiding in the tent so that the local Pakistani authorities would not try to stop him before he crossed over the border with the mujahideen. I explained that we were not just tourists but had also been visiting my father's charity project in Peshawar. When he heard my father's name, Rory relaxed and told us that he was not actually a doctor (and obviously not French), but he was in fact taking money into Panjshir for Afghanaid projects (run by Juliet) so he had to be careful that no one knew what he was doing as the news would spread and he could be robbed or stopped on the way in. He said it was terrible masquerading as a doctor as all the Afghans had been visiting him to demand he treat them and all he could do was distribute a small stock of aspirin. He said the women in the tent next door were not at all impressed by his medical expertise! We laughed over this and then left shortly after, wishing him a safe journey but never expecting to bump into him again.

More than a year later I returned to Peshawar – this time to work. The resilience and courage of the Afghan refugees that I had met in Garam Chasma on that trip had inspired me to go back to work in Peshawar as a volunteer. I met Juliet soon after my arrival. She came to visit me for tea – having been instructed by various people to check me out – her family knew my mother's family. Juliet remarked on the fact that I produced teacups with saucers in a very English way! Juliet was very charming and chatty but I remember feeling very intimidated. I had just spent the last few years backpacking around various parts of the world while Juliet had been busy running cross-border aid programmes from Pakistan into Afghanistan for Afghanaid and grappling with a complicated political and humanitarian situation.

After this first meeting in November 1988 I got to know Juliet well and eventually Rory as well. Despite different disasters that she suffered, Juliet was as resilient and brave as the Afghans she knew so well. I remember going out riding with her in Peshawar and seeing how she would laugh when her horse reared or ran away with her, just as an Afghan would. We used to ride out across the canal in University Town into fields of sugar cane with huge ditches on either side. Juliet would then gallop off and the rest of us would have to follow – sending farmers and their livestock diving for the ditches. It was quite terrifying!

Many years later, after 2001, Juliet came to visit us first in Peshawar and then in Kabul – the children were always fascinated by her eye patch and her stories. She brought lots of books for them to read – *The Silver Sword* and the Redwall series. The last time she came, Juliet set off to ride across Badakhshan and the Wakhan to cross the border into Pakistan above Chitral with friends and Fynn. None of us thought she would be permitted to cross over but she charmed the border guards and called a few friends in high places in Islamabad and was allowed to go down to Chitral.

A love of adventure, Afghans and animals – that is how I remember Juliet.

Buzkashi
Mary Crawley (I)

They were living in Peshawar, and she had three Afghan stallions tethered in the garden, tied up to trees. It was chaos when they got loose. Rory had just returned from filming the cruise missiles flying over and crashing into the palaces of Baghdad in the first Gulf War. On his return, she and Rory went for a ride. She put Rory on one of these stallions, she rode the other one and they raced off. Everything was done at full gallop. It had been raining and, with Julie leading the way, they went flat out round a corner and her horse slipped on the wet ground and fell, knocking itself out. But Julie had a broken back. Rory got her into a pick-up truck and to hospital, where she was examined. Rory spent the twenty thousand he had earned filming on flying Julie back from Peshawar to London, where she spent six weeks in the Royal London Hospital.

We did get to know Rory in the end. He knew what he wanted, but he was very charming, and he always looked after us – a bit more than Julie did! The last time I was in Peshawar, I had said to her, 'Before I go back, I'd like to see a game of *buzkashi*.' So she got her *chowkidar* to take me. That was fine. But after showing me where to stand, he said that he'd return for me in half an hour or so. I was left alone, obviously English and not native at all, surrounded by Afghans. In these situations, I say, 'Right, I'm going to be fine.' And I was. The game was tremendously exciting and there are no boundaries to the field so is quite likely to come to where you are standing – and everyone then gets out of the way. Although in *buzkashi* one team plays against another, they are also playing for themselves as really you want to be the one who scores and carries the dead goat over the goal line. It is played with a beheaded goat and there are very vicious little horses that all fight each other too.

A Focused Pirate

Carlotta Gall

Carlotta is a journalist, currently working for the New York Times.

Juliet was always the flag-bearer for me. I first met her in London with my father when she was back on a visit from Peshawar with her first husband Dominique. Dominique was bearded and tough-looking and had just been travelling inside Afghanistan – dangerous and difficult since this was during the Russian occupation – and Juliet had arranged for us to hear his news. It was one of her great talents, hooking people up, networking, communicating, always with a funny story but a driven focus on what was important.

My next memory was years later. Juliet had survived the sad loss of Dominique and was still working and living in her wonderful house in Peshawar with its garden filled with animals – horses, dogs, even a camel. One of the dogs was a huge *kuchi* hound, the type that nomadic herders use to guard their sheep and fight off wolves as they camp in the mountains and pastures, moving with the seasons. The dog was brought out as a puppy from Afghanistan by an aid worker and grew to a huge size but he was even more gentle and loyal than a Labrador. Fynn was small enough to ride on his back as on a pony and once cut off jagged clumps of his soft pale fur with a pair of scissors, an attention that the dog accepted without demur.

I was staying with my sister Fiona in Peshawar then and one day Juliet invited us over. We sat on her huge comfortable sofas amid Afghan cushions, flipping through her glossy magazines – we were starved for such things in Peshawar but trust Juliet to have the latest issues of *Tatler* and *Vogue*. I think there was champagne and Russian caviar too and Juliet announced we were celebrating since she and Rory had just got married. Bruce Wannell was there too and had been a witness at the church, and a few others. We were astounded and joyous – and to top it all they had been married by the Catholic priest Father Len – 'Don't tell my parents,' Juliet said with a carefree laugh – but they could not have made a better choice to take their vows. Father Len was a legendary kind and wise figure who oversaw the Christian community in Peshawar and was a great friend to Juliet.

The next time I caught up with Juliet was a time of great sadness in Moscow some months after Rory's death. She

Juliet and Rory's wedding party, Peshawar. L to R: Peter Jouvenal, Juliet, Rory and Joseph, the dog whose bite caused the bandage on her hand

was back in Moscow to pack up the house – a dacha in the forest near Boris Pasternak's former home on the outskirts of Moscow. I was in Moscow doing a brief internship at ITN. In her usual style she hosted a large candlelit dinner party for ten or twenty people and offered me her horses to ride. One of the horses, Light Brownie, an able Russian showjumper, was shipped back to England and spent his quarantine at our home in Penshurst, where he of course jumped out of his field. The dogs came back to England too. Juliet was calm and brave – she had had her eye operation by then also – but I remember taking the suburban train back into Moscow after seeing her depart and could not stop the tears streaming down my face.

She came back through Moscow less than a year later to work on the war in Chechnya; it was a horrendous war as the Russian military bludgeoned the Chechens under indiscriminate bombing. A lot of us covered that war but I was glad when after one tour Juliet pulled back from that depraved ugliness.

Juliet and Rory's wedding party. Yahya with the Gall sisters, Carlotta and Fiona

I saw her on and off over the years and her indomitable spirit was as strong as ever – on holiday in Maine with Fynn and Lettice, breezing through fractious family relations to welcome me; at Fiona and Philippe's wedding in Penshurst – where she stood out in a ruffled redingote and black eye patch, stifling a smile as a child whispered in awe at the pirate in our midst. She passed through too as the occasional guest in Kabul and perhaps the last time I saw her was when she was showing Fynn Afghanistan and heading up into the Wakhan corridor with him and friends for an epic ride across the Pamir mountains and down into Pakistan – undaunted by the fact that the border was closed. She made it through of course, with her entourage. Juliet was never the one to limp home defeated. She led her life to the full and set a great example – loving and living every adventure that life offers. It is certainly how I remember her.

Some Degree of Risk

Vladimir Snegirev

*Vladimir is a journalist and historian who wrote a book,
Ryzhii, about Rory Peck, whom he met filming the Russian–
Afghan war in Afghanistan.*

UNIVERSITY TOWN, PESHAWAR IN 1990

In Peshawar, any European woman who had no physical
disability looked pretty good. But Juliet could be considered
a beauty without any reservations – she had a slim athletic
figure; slightly quizzical blue-grey eyes; thin sensual lips; a
strong jaw and a shock of short-cropped chestnut hair. There
was something decisive in the appearance of this elegant
young lady. You immediately saw that she knew both her own
value and that of the world around her.

In the second half of the 1980s, Juliet ran the Peshawar
office of Afghanaid. When Rory worked briefly for the
charity, he met with her on business: together they did
the accounts, discussed plans and talked about everything
and nothing. Juliet, despite her youth, had spent almost
four years in the frontline city, and looked at Rory almost
condescendingly. So many of these people came from
London – they would stay for a week, turn out a paper and,
with obvious relief, return home. However, this Irishman
seemed different.

Very soon he told her that he was abandoning his work

at Afghanaid to devote himself entirely to filibustering as a freelance journalist.

From then on, Juliet rarely saw Rory. He vanished into Afghanistan for a long time, and when he returned to Peshawar, he was endlessly 'delayed' at the American Club. It was rumoured that he had a number of girlfriends.

Yet, when their paths crossed, he was always attentive and polite. One day, after returning home from a party, she commented on this laughingly to her husband. But her husband Dominique did not laugh with her.

'Yes, he's clearly in love with you. You'll see, if something ever happens to me, he'll make you an offer.' Juliet just laughed and said that he was inventing things.

Juliet had come to Peshawar as representative director of Afghanaid. She reviewed dossiers on the various regions of Afghanistan for the UN. This material was used to predict the number of potential refugees. She took part in anti-drug programmes; controlled the distribution of money coming in from around the world for the poor Afghans. Most of the funds came from the US. Officially they were supposed to be spent on food, but what the mujahideen actually spent them on was impossible to check.

Dominique Vergos had entered her life almost immediately after she arrived in Peshawar. He was considered a veteran here. At one point, Dominique had been a successful fashion photographer in Paris. Then he began to roam the 'hot spots' – Beirut, Africa, South East Asia. He knew how to take good pictures and sell them profitably. When turmoil broke out in Afghanistan, he settled near the war and quickly made friends with the commanders of guerrilla groups, almost becoming the official photographer of the jihad. Orders flooded in and he roamed through the mountains for months with the mujahideen. He learned to speak Farsi and Pashto. Once, he spent almost a year in guerrilla camps in Afghanistan.

However, unlike most other journalists, Dominique had another, secret life. A diplomat friend introduced him in Peshawar to some heavyweight American guys who suggested he might like to do something more useful while he was wandering around Afghanistan. The photographer didn't have to be persuaded. The Frenchman lived with his daughter from his first marriage, and his son by a girlfriend. He was fifteen years older than Juliet and resembled an extravagant rake, with tousled hair, demonic eyes and a free manner. Such people are rare. They follow their own path, outside accepted norms and laws. Perhaps it was this which drew her to him. He seemed talented and innovative. Even his relationship with US intelligence, which Dominique told her about in strict secrecy one day, worked in his favour, and gave him an air of mystery. She married him, and gave him a son, whom they called Fynn. They rented a beautiful villa in the University part of Peshawar on Circle Road, bringing servants and buying horses. Life was turning out remarkably well. However, sometimes something would come over him. After drinking, he would say that at any moment he might die, that then Juliet was sure to become a victim of this crazy Irishman … but in the morning, sober, he never mentioned it.

For two years, the idyll continued. But one day, it was all over.

Later, Juliet remembered how one day at a party, a French diplomat acquaintance warned Dominique to be careful: 'There are people who don't want you to be here.'

But Dominique only joked: 'You mean Najibullah agents? If I think about them all the time I'll go mad.'

'My job is to warn you,' shrugged the diplomat. 'I just received the information, so I strongly recommend you take some safety measures.'

At home, Juliet asked why he might be in danger.

'God, my darling, you know what I do. My job involves some degree of risk. That's why they pay me.'

'But this man meant something specific.'

'Unlikely. Someone, somewhere, said something ... and it spread.'

Juliet continued to insist: 'Think about where the threat might come from.'

'Well, perhaps from Gulbuddin. I never hid my opinion of him. His actions are destructive. They undermine the general struggle. Recently I spoke about it with the Americans. It could leak. Gulbuddin shows no mercy to his enemies.'

'Dominique – maybe we should leave.'

'It's just a guess. One of many. Just forget it. It'll blow over.'

But it didn't blow over. That evening they returned home late after dinner at the American Club. Juliet went straight to bed, but Dominique went to the garden to calm the dog which was barking at something. When Juliet heard machine-gunfire from her bed, she didn't attach any importance to it – shooting in Peshawar was common. Then an Afghan friend who lived nearby telephoned.

'Sorry it's so late. Where's Dominique?'

'Out in the garden. Why?'

'Go and check. I'm worried that he's in trouble.'

She threw a robe on and rushed outside. Dominique lay next to the house of their security guard. He was dead.

A neighbour ran over, saying that the Pashtun guard came to him and confessed that he killed his master. According to the Pushtun, Dominique was very drunk, burst into the guard house, and demanded that he give him a gun. Out of fright the guard shot him through the door. Through the door? But Dominique was killed by a bullet to the head. No, there was something wrong ...

The murderer was arrested. Juliet herself suggested that he be judged according to the laws of the free Pushtu tribes – such practices existed in Peshawar. They gathered the elders.

Their verdict was unanimous – the man was guilty, and deserved severe punishment. Either he should be executed, or there should be a large financial compensation – the widow should choose.

She would make the choice, but who could help her solve the mystery of the murder? Juliet promised herself that, sooner or later, she would find out the truth.

***

Amazingly, Dominique's prediction about the Irishman came true almost as soon as Juliet became herself again. A year passed. No, Rory was not intrusive, and when they met behaved like a gentleman. He sent cards and flowers; he offered help. He regularly invited her to spend the evening with him at the American Club.

Rory abandoned his many girlfriends. Previously he had liked to carouse around, especially after returning from war, washing off the dust and dirt and dressing as usual once more – blood bubbled in his veins. But now things were different.

When Juliet began to respond with smiles, a dance in a bar, a leisurely conversation over the phone, he lost his head completely. Rory suggested that they live together; she asked him to be patient – she had promised herself never to marry again and she didn't have the strength to start all over again.

In late 1990, Juliet came to London to sit exams to work for the Foreign Office. They had been asking her to do so for some time.

Rory called her from Baghdad – where war was already erupting – to ask her to dinner. They had dinner by candlelight at the Capital Hotel in London, and left the hotel four days later. When they bumped into a friend after this lengthy 'dinner', he took one glance at this wonderful couple, and immediately ordered champagne.

'How serious is it, Juliet?' he asked, when Rory had left the room.

She shrugged: 'In two days he is going to Moscow, and I to Pakistan. I just don't know.'

But the next morning, Rory sought out Juliet in the Foreign Office building, invited her to lunch, and there, very, very seriously, put a wedding ring on her finger.

Ten days later he called her in Peshawar and asked her to come immediately to Moscow. For some reason Rory was set on getting married in Russia.

Bruce Clarke would arrange everything, he said.

Poor Bruce! You should have seen his face when he found out that he was the one to arrange it. Much smaller problems flustered him. And now he had to arrange the marriage of two UK citizens, Protestants, and Rory categorically insisted on a church ceremony. What Orthodox priest would marry Protestants? Bruce was close to despair. But Rory waved his hand nonchalantly.

'Is there a Georgian church here?'

'There is,' replied Bruce, uncertainly, 'not far from the zoo.'

'Then everything is fine. I think the Georgians would marry savages if it was for money.'

They found the church, and at the entrance encountered a tipsy sacristan.

'Just what we need!' said Rory, delightedly.

But the church priest rejected the foreigner's assertive proposal. He would not help – not even promises of a generous reward to the church would sway him.

'It would be easier to send you to the moon, than do this,' he told them straight.

Rory looked momentarily confused.

'Let's go back to Peshawar.'

But even there they met with failure: the vicar of the Anglican church, hearing of Rory's divorce, also threw them out. Rory didn't give up. Eventually, he found a Catholic priest, who was more accommodating. This glorious Italian was not troubled by the Protestant faith of the young couple, or the previous family history of the groom. He saw how touchingly Rory looked at Juliet, how they clung to each other's hands, and agreed.

Peter [Jouvenal] told me that it was the most hilarious wedding he had ever been to. Rory wanted there to be organ music at the ceremony. But the organ in this church was so decrepit that no one wanted to play it. They finally persuaded a guy from Afghanaid, who had played music as a child. He sat down, hit the keys, and almost half of them fell off at once. The organ began to make strange sounds which were completely inappropriate for the solemn moment. Peter could barely restrain his laughter. The priest kept his stiff upper lip. He continued the ceremony, as expected. The young couple exchanged rings. Then everyone went to Juliet's house, where Peter photographed the happy couple and made a toast.

Much later, Juliet confessed to me: 'As soon as we became friends, I knew that we would be together, that this day must come, because Rory and I loved the same things. The dream of ninety-nine per cent of my friends has been a secure and quiet life in England. Rory wanted something different. He lived for risk, for this life, which demanded everything from him.'

MOSCOW SUBURBS; THE DACHA IN PEREDELKINO, 1993

'Vladimir, tell me, do you like black caviar?'

'What a stupid question! Of course I do.'

'Then come over with Tanya this evening. We'll have lots of Irish whiskey and black caviar.'

'Tanya!' I shouted to my wife, hanging up the phone, 'tonight we're going to the Pecks' in Peredelkino.'

My British friend had arranged his life in Moscow exactly how he wanted it. I laughed at him when he spoke about a manor with stables. Yet, extraordinarily, he found a comfortable home in a prestigious suburban village, got two horses, dogs, and even mentioned Juliet's desire to have a camel – although why they wanted a camel, I didn't understand.

Peredelkino has always been home to famous writers

and poets. The mere fact that Pasternak worked there for many years gave the village a special status. It was clear that for Rory, this significance was also important – he would never live somewhere horrible.

Yet this was a good place in its own right. Some fifteen miles from the Kremlin you fall under the shadow of century-old pine trees in the sleepy quiet of the charming cottages of the Moscow suburbs. In the vast grounds, surrounded by a wooden fence, stood a two-storey house: downstairs was a living room with a fireplace, office and a terrace, upstairs three bedrooms. There was an old, rather neglected garden, which Juliet tried in vain to convert into a real English lawn, and a dilapidated barn which she turned into a stable.

Life was good in Peredelkino. They brought up their children. A cat and two shaggy dogs seemed to materialise: an amiable sheepdog from the Caucasus which they named Brezhnev, and a slobbering bulldog, called Boris – in honour of Yeltsin, perhaps. In the morning the children climbed into their parents' bed, and Rory served tea. Then they went for a walk in the forest. Of course, this only happened on days when he was free. Very often, Rory was sent off by different TV companies to 'hot spots' which appeared every now and then in the former Soviet Union. He filmed a civil war in Tajikistan; fierce fighting between Georgians and Abkhazians in the Caucasus; and travelled to Nagorno-Karabakh … then Yugoslavia flared up, and Rory filmed there.

Increasingly his wife travelled with him, quickly learning the duties of an assistant and producer.

He still spent all his money with ease and lived not thinking about tomorrow. Sometimes conversation turned to India, where they had once planned to go.

'Wait a little longer,' Rory would say, 'Soon everything will calm down here, there won't be any more work, and then we will go.'

A (rather hopeful) valentine from Rory to Juliet

In India he wanted to buy a tea plantation, abandon his dangerous life for good, settle down and become a respectable planter. Juliet only smiled back thinly, replying, 'So you say, darling.'

In the evenings or at the weekend they invited friends to stay. Rory bought a crazy amount of black caviar, which at that time in Moscow was worth pennies if you had hard cash. Juliet put the caviar on the table, cutting large slices of French baguettes and slathering them with butter, and happily we ate it all, washing it down with red wine and whiskey. Sometimes Rory cooked a leg of lamb, working his magic on a special gravy, and Juliet cooked Pakistani rice. For some reason this was the only thing he allowed her to cook.

When a loud cry suddenly came from their little daughter, Lettice, upstairs, Juliet paid absolutely no attention. Not batting an eyelid, she sweetly smiled at her guests, continued her conversation and poured more wine. My Tanya was astonished: she leaps up as soon as our own child opens its mouth.

'That is why the British grow up so independent,' I told her, 'from infancy they learn that they have to rely on themselves.' She nodded, but couldn't understand.

On the fire, birch logs burned brightly, upstairs children yelled, snow fell outside the windows. Brezhnev watched the guests complacently from a shabby armchair; Boris gnawed at the table legs. Rory gazed lovingly at Juliet, and looked the picture of a domesticated chap. He would even wear slippers and pyjamas. Then he invited everyone for a walk. We took our glasses of wine, threw on our jackets, and walked among the pines, talking of nothing in particular.

The evenings were glorious.

Translated from the Russian by Lettice Crawley Peck and Julia Dvinskaya

MOSCOW

They Breathed Different Air
Bruce Clark

Bruce Clark is a writer-at-large, and the online religion editor, for the Economist. *He also lectures on a range of subjects, including early Christian history, forced migrations in the twentieth century and the story of textiles.*

B eing a correspondent during the dying days of the Soviet Union was a professional experience like no other, by turns fascinating, exhausting and terrifying. Moscow was a city of decaying buildings, empty shops and cross people whose old lives were collapsing. Hours were long, editors were demanding, communications with London very hard.

On top of the general difficulties of life, each of us had particular problems and insecurities. I had come to Moscow for a precarious start-up newspaper which had no office or accommodation in the city, and I had to migrate perpetually from one hotel room or primitive flat to another. I then moved over to *The Times*, without ever working at its London office or fully understanding my new masters' demands, which were unpredictable and never-ending.

In the midst of this frustrating existence, there appeared two people who seemed to breathe different air. Not the freezing blasts, laced with cheap petrol, that pervaded Moscow, but some other grade of oxygen. First, my old friend Rory: no longer the engagingly wild party animal I remembered from

Ireland but an accomplished cameraman, still keen to live life on the edge but with a new sense of purpose after some chastening years in Afghanistan. And then Juliet, who shared his panache, his penchant for the exotic and perilous, and his impatience with all things petty and hypocritical.

I was fast asleep in one of my Moscow eyries when Rory rang me, from a distant location and at a strange hour: he urgently needed Russian visas for two British subjects, a Mrs Juliet Vergos and her toddler son Fynn, mainly resident in Peshawar. Soon there was another request: he wanted to marry Juliet, urgently, and he asked me to investigate the possibilities in Moscow. I did explore a few options, including a Georgian Orthodox priest who replied that flying to the moon would be easier for him than conjoining two stray Anglicans. In the end, they married in Pakistan, shortly before Rory went to Baghdad to cover the American bombardment of that city. This was January 1991.

Soon Juliet appeared in Russia, and they made Moscow their home. This was the very end of the period when all accommodation for expatriates was controlled by a Soviet government agency. Foreigners were beginning to make private rental deals, in a grey legal area. Living space of any kind was hard to come by.

But this didn't bother Rory or Juliet. They initially found a small, rather dingy flat in a modern building near the central Moscow ring road, and even that unpromising premises became a place of fun and hospitality. It was conveniently close to a farmers' market; where prices were high for Russian pockets but dollars went a long way. Juliet quickly learned to convey her wishes in sign language. She and Rory discovered an unlimited source of caviar, and that became a standard feature of all their entertaining. But Rory was not satisfied. From the moment he turned up in Moscow, he told me he wanted to live in style, in the countryside; I said the rules made that utterly impossible, but Rory was not impressed by rules.

Sure enough, he and Juliet found a lovely wooden cottage with a decent-sized garden in Peredelkino, a village on the outskirts of Moscow where favoured Soviet writers were allowed to live. That was the start of what seemed, to friends like me, like a charmed existence. In contrast with some newlyweds, theirs was a kind of happiness which they wanted to share. They made themselves comfortable and entertained with great generosity. They hired Russian staff to help look after Fynn and Lettice, who was born in January 1992. There was handsome Genna, a driver who took Fynn to school, plus garrulous Galina and strong-willed Ira who took care of the baby.

They acquired horses and built up a collection of kitschy Soviet art to add to their Afghan mementoes. An invitation to their household portended a delicious, candlelit meal, with Edith Piaf tapes in the background and war stories that grew more lively as the alcohol flowed. Or in the daytime, a long

Rory and Lettice on Light Brownie, Peredelkino 1993

walk over winding snowy paths where you half expected to run into a resurrected Pasternak or Chekhov. They discovered one of Moscow's best riding-schools, and we would go for some enjoyable early-morning canters over open fields with James Mates, who is now an ITN news reader, and our Polish colleague, Ewa Ewart. For me, these were enjoyable interludes in an otherwise pretty tough existence.

And Rory and Juliet paid an even higher price for their home comforts. Every so often, the two of them would make a joint excursion to some troubled place on the exploding Soviet periphery: Georgia, Azerbaijan, Moldova, or a bit further afield to the war zones of Bosnia. Rory would gather news footage to sell to the highest bidder and Juliet would act as his assistant. There were jokes about Juliet's determination to remain elegant even in the most hazardous moments. In a Bosnian city full of snipers, she used the mirror of an armoured car to check her lipstick, or so the story went.

Lettice and Lenin, Peredelkino, 1993

In retrospect, many might say it was not very sensible for the two of them to be incurring so much danger simultaneously. Couldn't they have taken turns, at least, to keep the home fires burning? But both were following a powerful calling to seek out, explore and document the world's most troubled places. Rory was playing for high stakes, but not recklessly. He was prepared to shoulder risks, but only if the reward, in the form of information and images from an important place, made that worthwhile. On those matters, Juliet and he understood one another perfectly.

Moscow and the crumbling Russian empire were an environment where so many strange, near-impossible things kept happening that you needed a lively, unconventional mind to keep abreast of things. To survive psychologically, you had to be able to find humour and happiness amidst all the turmoil. Juliet and Rory had all those virtues in abundance. With their converging qualities, they created a little Muscovite world that was both magical and very real. Around them, you sometimes felt as though you were entering a film script, except there was nothing forced, affected or phony about the way they lived. They were being true to their wild and wonderful selves. Their favourite song was 'Je ne regrette rien'.

A Trek in Mongolia
Juliet Crawley Peck

This is an amalgamated extract of two pieces found among Juliet's papers about a family trip to Mongolia. The piece begins on the journey from Irkutsk to Ulan Bator.

The train was teeming with Mongolians who were cramming luggage and merchandise into every available corner. A very drunk Russian conductress was engaged in a bitter struggle with a young man who was attempting to hide large rolls of plastic sheeting in the loo. Despite giving him a bloody nose, they evidently came to some agreement, because after we had been through customs, he and numerous other Mongolian businessmen were seen, grinning broadly, carrying them and other enormous bags, out of her compartment and back down the train. Apart from the initial fight, the boys were not interested in seeing firsthand this movement of contraband. Instead they were busy making friends with Ken, a middle-aged American businessman in the next-door compartment, who gave them his metal disc visiting cards which jumped when put on cold stone. The boys took handfuls, and were to leave them scattered across the endless steppe.

After two days in a cramped compartment, we staggered out on to the platform in Ulan Bator, wondering where the legend of romantic travel on the Trans-Siberian Railway originated. We were in time for the *Nadam*, an annual

Mongolian national festival of wrestling, archery and horse-racing which dates back to the time of Ghengis Khan. The fighting techniques of the wrestlers were studied intensely and later used in interfraternal squabbles, though the strange victory dance which imitates the flight of a bird was regarded as too sissy to be of use. More popular was the horse-racing. About two hundred and fifty ponies ran a distance of one *urton* (about thirty kilometres), ridden by children as young as five, wearing what appeared to be bishops' mitres with their numbers on. The races lasted about two hours. The boys galloped – many bareback – down the steppe to the finish, whooping and shouting, beating their exhausted horses, to be scooped up by fathers and elder brothers who then retrieved the horses with a lasso.

We had planned to go the next day. But Bold, our trusted guide, refused to let us leave for another twenty-four hours, because it was a Tuesday, according to Mongolians an inauspicious day for departure.

We spent this time exploring Ulan Bator, a city suffering from some of the worst effects of Soviet architectural disability. Built principally in the last sixty years, it is a typical example of the cheap, ugly, residential style, with endless monotonous high-rise apartments in poor repair. Serious planning faults have led to the placing of power stations and factories within the city centre, which in turn has led to severe pollution problems. But there are some fine buildings around the central Sukhbaatar Square, including the state opera and ballet theatre. The highlight was the somewhat dusty central museum, which housed a magnificent collection of dinosaur remains, including a skeleton of a Tyrannosaurus Rex. The boys were impressed, and were determined to find their own dinosaur bones on the trek – which led to many conflicts with the drivers who protested when yet more camel bones were stowed away in the truck.

On Wednesday morning we were ready to go. Despite strict instructions on minimalism, with all the cricket bats, footballs, fishing rods and riding equipment, we had accumulated a fearsome amount of luggage. This was piled, along with three weeks of provisions, into two jeeps and a truck. We also had a *ger*, a traditional Mongolian circular felt tent. We had originally planned to use the *ger* every night, but because it took nearly two hours to erect we soon detected a marked reluctance to put it up for a one-night stop, and in the last week it was announced to be strangely and inexplicably 'broken'. Travelling with us were three drivers, one cook, two *ger* 'experts' and Dundee Bold, our guide, so named for his apparent similarity to the character played by Paul Hogan and the need to differentiate him from 'cook' Bold.

It was the beginning of seven days of almost continuous rain. This was to be the wettest summer in Mongolia for twenty-five years. We had planned to travel in a wide circle. To

Mongolia. Fynn, Jamie, Ali and Rory

drive first to the mountains in the north-west where we would pick up horses on which we would trek south, reaching some way into the Ghobi desert. There we would change to camels for ten days before turning back to Ulan Bator. But with only 1,300 kilometres of macadam road in the entire country, sixty kilometres west of Ulan Bator we were on dirt tracks. The rain made these particularly difficult. We swayed and bumped over the mountain trails, crossing swollen rivers on precarious wooden bridges, and when these had been washed away, driving extensive detours. The jeeps were in such poor condition that we had at least two punctures and one breakdown daily. My husband, determined that no moment should be lost, drilled the boys on their multiplication tables and gave impromptu history and French lessons. They were soon well versed in British military superiority, the hopelessness of the French army and the looming Japanese threat.

In the evenings, we would pitch camp beside a lake or stream where the boys would optimistically fish and search for dinosaur bones. We taught the Mongolians cricket. The novelty of the game intrigued them, but a reluctance to catch the ball and an insistence on holding the bat as in American baseball somewhat hampered any real development of skill. In return they taught us *sol*, a form of volleyball, which was to prove much more popular with all.

The vastness and emptiness of the country is staggering. We passed rolling pastureland and low mountains covered with a sea of blue and yellow flowers. The mixed fragrance of thyme and onion grass is pervasive. Occasionally, we came across a herd of cattle or horses and sometimes some arable land from a disintegrating collective farm. We rarely met another vehicle.

Away from the cities, there are of course no restaurants or hotels, but the hospitality of rural Mongolians is legendary. We seldom passed a *ger* without stopping for refreshing bowls of *kumiss*, fermented mare's milk, which has a slightly bitter and tangy taste and is the nomads' summer fare. We were always warmly welcomed, although I'm sure that many times these patient people must have inwardly groaned at having to be polite to such a large party.

The children had the usual schoolboys' attitude to foreign food. They complained endlessly at the soup and noodles which made up our main diet, and went to great lengths to avoid eating them. We were, however, determined that they should learn and experience at any cost. This food war raged throughout the holiday, with neither side giving any quarter.

The majority of *gers* belonged to nomads who, with the fall of Communism, had left their collective farms to herd privately. As far as possible they were self-supporting, buying only flour, rice, material and medical supplies from the local towns. The range of their movements depended entirely on the weather, some travelled as little as two kilometres in the winter, whilst others might travel two or three hundred.

We visited the sixteenth-century monastery at Karakorum which has been virtually closed since 1937. Zondai Tonda, a seventy-year-old lama, who was too young to be purged by the Communists, told us that: 'The worst years of the persecution were from 1934 to 1939. During this time all lamas between the ages of seventeen and ninety were taken away. They were never seen again.' Buddhism though is currently undergoing a revival with one hundred and forty new monasteries opening in the last three years. Erten Bat, one of our drivers, preferred to visit a local lama when suffering from inflammation of the throat, putting his trust in the monotonous chanting of prayers and passing burning incense around his body, rather than the meagre medical supplies of the deteriorating state health system.

After a week of driving in the rain, we decided to head south on the principle that the Ghobi desert should at least be dry. Feeling rather ashamed of ourselves, we stopped at the tourist camp at Hushiert, where we revelled in hot showers, dry beds and warm stoves in our holiday *gers*. The boys bought Snickers and Coca Cola at enormously inflated prices in the 'duty free shop' and declared that at last they were enjoying themselves. In the evening we sat in the dining room, an enormous *ger* worthy of the Golden Horde, and listened to a group of Italian tourists serenading thirty Japanese factory workers with renderings from the *Sound of Music* and *Dolce Vita*. This, and the timely arrival of the sun, set us speeding on our way the following morning, having exchanged our jeeps for horses.

The Mongolian horses were an immediate success. No more than twelve hands, they are exceedingly tough and resilient. In winter they survive temperatures of -35° without apparent difficulty. Within two days, the boys were galloping over the steppe, Ali shouting 'I'm the Duke of Wellington', and Fynn as Jessie James in hot pursuit. 'Bang, Bang! You're dead, you're dead.' 'No I'm not, I ducked.'

Mongolians stand in their saddles and it is very obvious why. They are exceedingly uncomfortable. But standing requires strong knees. The result of all this was that by the end of the first day all of the grown-ups were in complete agony, and stuffing any extra jumper or jacket beneath them to ease the pain. The children were more resilient; they galloped round their poor parents in a continual show of superiority.

Whatever we suffered on the ponies was nothing in comparison to what we endured on the camels. We collected these some thirty kilometres into the Ghobi. They looked a pretty motley lot, still shedding their winter coats, humps sagging through lack of fat. Bold excused this by explaining that camels are generally used only in the autumn and winter. These camels did not appreciate the interruption of their summer grazing, and they were in a foul temper.

It is impossible to find anything positive to say about these frightful creatures. They bite, spit, kick, smell, and rarely do what they are told. One day in the saddle is enough to transform one into a physical wreck and one night was enough to teach us to camp upwind. The smell is vile.

The terrain of the Ghobi is varied. The children had hoped for long stretches of sand, but these were further south than we ventured. We were continually being told that we would see sand 'over the next range of hills', but one by one our party gave up the struggle, and reverted to walking or travelling by vehicle. After six days we had had enough and with great relief returned to that miracle of modern transportation, the Russian jeep.

On the last day in the Ghobi we bought a goat from a family in whose *ger* we were resting. To the fascination of the children it was summarily killed, by the plucking out of its heart. Within an hour, the blood and fat were being packed

Mongolia. Juliet, Fynn, Ali, Rory and Jamie

into the intestines for black pudding, and the meat was being boiled by dropping burning coals into a milk churn full of water. Everyone in the vicinity was invited in to enjoy this variation to the normal diet, a change not greatly appreciated by many in our family.

We turned north and collected some more horses for part of the return lap. We visited the rocky outcrop where the Mongolian equivalent to Robin Hood is said to have lived and we travelled through dramatic mountain scenery. We rode up through river valleys, over passes covered with edelweiss and other alpine flowers to high mountain plateaus with views stretching for miles. At one time we counted as many as nine hawks, hovering motionless above us in the brilliant, blue sky.

For reasons of its inaccessibility Mongolia must be one of the very few unspoiled countries left in the world. I have rarely travelled anywhere in the East where the people are so unobtrusive and respectful of other people's beliefs. No one attempted to convert me to Buddhism, or insisted on tedious and futile political arguments. Particularly in the rural areas, I felt that the people had a deep love and respect for their heritage, and they had none of the complexes so often found when East meets West, only a polite interest for something they obviously believe will never concern them directly.

Altai adventure
Harriet Crawley

Harriet has stood both for the UK and the European Parliaments. Based in Moscow, she was agent for a Russian landscape photographer, and then, until this year, worked for the oil and gas industry. She is currently working on a novel. Harriet's father and Juliet's grandfather were first cousins.

The first time I ever set foot in Russia was in 1992 and my first night under a Russian sky was in Juliet's cramped Soviet-style apartment somewhere near Kievsky station. We went to the market and bought a kilo of caviar for about twenty pounds which we spread thickly over fresh white bread and gorged ourselves in Juliet's spartan kitchen, washing down the black nectar with vodka. At some point that evening Bruce Clark arrived and joined in the feast. Rory was in Chechnya, and telephoned that evening. Juliet was about to join him. Meanwhile baby Lettice and Fynn were tucked up in bed under the watchful eye of a Russian nanny.

It was wonderful to see Juliet happy again. Always beautiful and stylish, on that evening she was light-hearted and laughing. Rory had adopted Fynn, and now they had Lettice. Life was good, and exciting. The Moscow apartment was only temporary, Juliet explained. They had found a wooden dacha to rent in a village buried in thick woods just outside Moscow called Peredelkino. Juliet talked about bringing her horses to Peredelkino from Pakistan, so she could ride in the woods. As I listened to these plans between sips of vodka and mouthfuls of heavenly caviar, little did I realise that the dacha which Juliet and Rory would make their home for over a year would one day be my home, where I would live with Spencer, my son, and with Gleb, my Russian husband.

On 31 August 1994, Spencer, Gleb and I moved to a dacha in Peredelkino close to Juliet's old home. By this time Rory had died and Juliet had left. Peredelkino was a wonderful spot, set deep in the pine forest. In our garden alone were one hundred and twenty pine trees soaring above the wooden house. Spencer went to a Russian school in Moscow, and at weekends played rudimentary ice hockey on a bumpy pitch which Gleb had made by flooding the lawn, or – and this was his favourite pastime – hurtled down the snow-covered lanes on his toboggan which we had tied with a rope to the back fender of my clapped-out Lada.

From my wonderful Russian neighbours, Tanya and Igor, I heard all about Juliet and her life in Peredelkino. They talked warmly about this beautiful young English woman who rode every day in the woods on one of her horses, and said that she was fearless and headed into the forest even in deepest winter. Igor, who was a scientist, told me how they had met: he and Tanya were walking down the alley outside their house, a deep rutted road cut deep into the forest and flanked on either side by dense pine trees, when a young woman came towards them with a couple of dogs by her side. Suddenly, from nowhere, a large Alsatian jumped out and growled at Juliet and her dogs. The young woman was completely unfazed. She went right up to the Alsatian, gripped its muzzle and opened its mouth, and declared that it was a young dog, and there was nothing to worry about … he was not dangerous. The Alsatian, no doubt as stunned as anyone, became docile, while Juliet introduced herself. In 2014 it was a great pleasure for me to bring Lettice to Peredelkino to meet Tanya and Igor and hear this story firsthand, and for Lettice to see where her mother and father had lived.

Another memory: it was sometime in 1994, after Rory had died, that Juliet appeared in Moscow, on her way to Chechnya which was still at war with Russia. She was writing an article about Russian soldiers killed in Chechnya whose bodies were not being returned to their families. Gleb and I took her to Vnukovo airport in the middle of the night to catch a flight to Grozny. She knew no fear.

I want to make a serious point about Juliet's love of far-flung places. It was not capricious. Living abroad, with a foreign language ringing in her ears, and dust rising from the road, was Juliet's way of understanding the world, breaking out of what she saw as the narrow confines of her immediate English circle. She was devoted to her parents and siblings but she sought a wider horizon, a bigger world, and she found it. Juliet had the highest admiration for Freya Stark and this passage, we both agreed, says it all:

Though it may be unessential to the imagination, travel is necessary to an understanding of men. Only with long experience and the opening of his wares on many a beach where his language is not spoken, will the merchant come to know the worth of what he carries, and what is parochial and what is universal in his choice. Such delicate goods as justice, love and honour, courtesy, and indeed all the things we care for, are valid everywhere; but they are variously moulded and often differently handled, and sometimes nearly unrecognizable if you meet them in a foreign land; and the art of learning fundamental common values is perhaps the greatest gain of travel to those who wish to live at ease among their fellows.

How well I remember Juliet railing at the parochialism she so often encountered in England. 'I am baffled when I hear some people say that you cannot be a good person if you are not a Christian. I know from my own experience that is *not true*!'

In 1995, we had moved into Juliet and Rory's old dacha in Peredelkino. Juliet stayed with us and she and I walked down the lanes where she had ridden in winter through the deep snow, and visited Tanya and Igor, and she invited other friends over for supper. Her courage in the face of another death, and of cancer in the eye, was extraordinary. But this I knew already. Only days after Rory had died, Juliet came to stay with me directly from Moscow ahead of the funeral. Then she was in shock. Now, two years later, she was dealing again with life vigorously, hopefully, grateful to have a new job which meant she could travel.

In the summer, Juliet joined Gleb, Spencer and me, and our beloved Franco Sersale, Spencer's godfather, on an epic journey to the Altai, an autonomous region in southern Russia, originally inhabited by indigenous tribes. I felt very protective towards Juliet on that trip, but of course my anxiety was misplaced. We flew from Moscow to Barnaul (four hours) and then took a thirteen-hour car journey deep into the Altai mountains to stay at a lake-side hotel which had electricity for two hours at a time, and a helicopter for tourists if you did not mind a pilot who was perpetually drunk. On the first evening we arrived, Juliet took a rowing boat by herself and rowed out into the lake. It was light almost until midnight and the water was like glass. All you heard was the soft splashing of her oars. I watched her and understood that she was wrapping herself in the beauty and the stillness of the moment. That night she talked about herself and her life without a trace of self-pity. 'I have my photographs and my memories and no one can take those from me.'

We eschewed the helicopter and opted for horses, and the next day we set off across a high plateau to look for Scythian graves. Grasslands stretched as far as the eye could see to a shimmering horizon of blue mountains; we stood at the apex of four countries: China, Kazakhstan, Mongolia and Russia. A strong wind whipped the tough tall grasses of the plain, and sent shadows racing, while kites soared high above. Our horses, however, were pitiful: under-fed and sluggish.

Out of nowhere a man on an impressive stallion and with a beautiful high saddle galloped up to us and introduced himself to our guide. He was an Altai big shot, head of a local tribe, and he was keen to show off his riding prowess by digging in his spurs and making his stallion rear up on its hind legs, not once but several times. Unexpectedly, he threw out a challenge which our guide translated: 'Do any of these foreigners want to race me across the plain?' I was amazed to hear Juliet respond, 'Yes, I will race you!' The next thing I knew she had shortened her stirrups and gathered up her reins, and when the guide shouted 'go' she gave her half-asleep horse a ferocious belt with a whip, and shot off across the plain.

Juliet was the most beautiful rider, but this race was perhaps her finest, given the dismal condition of her horse. She won by sheer willpower and brute force, whipping the horse to go faster and faster. Mr Big Shot was so furious he slunk away. I laughed and laughed while Juliet looked like the cat that had swallowed the cream. That girl had style. I miss her and always will.

A Dangerous Existence
Simon Crawley (II)

In Moscow, Rory and Julie had a dog, which looked like a husky, called Boris, after Boris Yeltsin who was premier at the time. The kennel that they kept him in was called the Kremlin. Julie employed a Russian nanny who was the daughter of a KGB general; she was horrified that the dog was called Boris and the kennel the Kremlin – she thought it was disrespectful. Julie's answer was, 'Well, my dog in England is called Thatcher. We think it is an honour.'

Moscow was their base, but the war was on in the Balkans, where they went on sorties. Once, they went to Sarajevo, and Rory managed to find somebody who would guide him over the mountains to Srebrenica. He filmed there and met Julie by arrangement several days later at Split. They worked together, mostly on a freelance basis: Rory would do the filming, and Julie would edit and then send it, via satellite dish, to any country that wanted it.

One day they had news that somebody important was arriving by plane at Sarajevo airport. To get to this airport you had to go across an open space, which was known as Snipers' Alley. Rory borrowed an armoured car and Kate Adie thumbed a lift. They came under fire and some of the bullets penetrated the armour. Kate Adie was hit. As soon as they got out of danger, Rory filmed Kate Adie's delicate ankle, which was blood-smeared.

We had an arrangement with the Foreign Office. If anything happened to Rory and Julie, we would be allowed to go to Moscow to pick up the children and bring them back here. For instance, there was a revolution and civil war going on in Georgia in late summer 1993. Western journalists, including Rory and Julie, were based in a seaside town called Sukhumi. I came in from visiting in the early evening to see a news flash. Mary was in the kitchen doing some ironing. There was a report that of the last three planes to fly out of Sukhumi, two had been shot down into the sea. It was understood that there were thirty-six Western journalists on board. Mary asked me whether it was time to pack our bags.

I suppose that we were always aware that something might happen. But you can't live on a knife-edge. Mary went off to take the Mothers' Union meeting, and I stayed in the Rectory. Julie knew that this report was being broadcast and rang us the same evening to say that she was all right and had got to Tbilisi.

Juliet with Lettice, Peredelkino, 1993

It was a dangerous existence. I suppose the only thing you can do is rely on prayer – nothing else is going to protect them. You don't become indifferent, but you can't think about it all the time. There were times Mary and I used to look after Fynn and Letty. I suppose, in some ways, it gave us something to concentrate on and be active about. We just lived, busy keeping life just ordinary life. But it wasn't particularly easy – there was this knowledge that Rory and Julie were often in danger, and that where there is fighting, you get hurt.

She had a faith, and it meant a lot to her. She used to go to the cathedral, I think, in Peshawar. She talked to me about her faith very little. She was very private and it was understood rather than spoken about. Priscilla and the two boys are busy exercising a ministry, but Julie didn't. In the time that we were living here and she had cancer, there was a bond of unspoken understanding that deepened. We knew that she believed and we had this basic trust. But faith was very real and important to her, and she really wanted it for her children. When she lived up here [in Yorkshire], she always used to take them up to the church on a Sunday – but it meant much more to her than that.

Grozny: No Ordinary Task

Vaughan Smith

After leaving the Grenadier Guards, Vaughan co-founded the news agency, Frontline Television, with Rory Peck and Peter Jouvenal in 1989. The following describes the weeks after President Yeltsin ordered the invasion of Grozny.

A couple of years after Rory died, Juliet came to Frontline to ask if she could renew her role in the agency. I was really pleased. Not only was she very smart and capable, there was also the link with Rory: we were all desperately cut up about losing him, and this was a way that we could involve her and support her – she needed to earn some money, particularly with two young children to look after.

It was the winter of 1994, and the Grozny story had started to pick up. We were planning to send out a fair few people, and we were worried about how to get their footage out – we were still filming on tapes in those days. We believed the agencies would all be outside the city, where we had to get the material to. We came to an arrangement with Juliet whereby she could take a percentage on all of our footage if she would resupply us, get our footage to the right people and aid the sales process. On that basis, she flew with us out there, allowing us to focus on filming.

Juliet based herself in Mineralnaya Voda, outside Grozny, where most of the other agencies were. She would approach the

BBC, AP, Reuters and DPA to tell them where Frontline was, ask them what stories they were doing and what they needed.

The BBC wanted to encourage the already close relationship it had with Frontline, so she was able to share its armoured vehicle (a Courtauld, a glass composite but light and quite nimble) to drive into Grozny. The trip would be triangular: they would resupply the BBC, come to resupply us, discuss what we wanted and take out our tape, then return to Mineralnaya Voda.

Although not alone, this was no ordinary task. Grozny means 'terrible' in Russian, an appropriate name from what we saw of it. Russian jets were bombing the Chechens – silent, by the time you had spotted them there were only seconds to leave the road or get out of the vehicle and hide in a ditch. In terms of intensity of conflict, it cannot have been unlike a major city under bombardment during WWII. Although we'd come in and out of the city by vehicle, we'd get away from the frontline by foot. As you walked away, you could hear the crunching of all the shattered glass underneath your feet, beneath the snow. When you dropped down to avoid further shelling, you'd cut your knees.

The route into Grozny that Juliet usually took – every other day, sometimes every day – crossed a partially damaged bridge. Half the road had been shelled and often the Russians would cover it with fire, so crossing was very dangerous. You couldn't hang around. Then she had to look for us, a crew of perhaps a dozen hairy and smelly journalists with no running water in some basement, for we might have moved. If we had, we would leave a note in our old place with a map of where we planned to be. She then had to negotiate the destroyed city to try to find us – if she took the wrong corner, the Russians could have blown her to bits.

There was no better person to do the job that she was doing: a female version of a guardsman, she was an exemplar of that typically English phlegmatic courage and one of the bravest women we knew.

Despite that, our relationship wasn't always an easy one. After Rory and she moved to Moscow, I felt that she wanted to sell his footage herself. Also, we didn't necessarily agree about Frontline's purpose. Although we were working hard and were where we should have been as freelancers, then as now, the freelance trade earns little or no money. She needed money, and the commissions that she received were not very good.

Despite that she was an exceptional individual. She was at her indomitable, courageous best in Grozny, supplying us and taking considerable risk in doing so – all for eight hundred quid, all in.

Juliet at work, possibly in Chechnya

Retreat from Moscow: The Drive to Smolensk

Christopher and Brigitte Granville

As a diplomat, Christopher served as First Secretary in the British Embassy in Moscow. He then co-founded Trusted Sources, an emerging markets and consultancy firm. While in Russia, Brigitte advised the Russian government on monetary policy; she now divides her time between her horses and being an Economics Professor at Queen Mary University of London.

During the 1990s, we lived in Moscow and there we met Juliet – for the first time, in November 1994, on the snow-bound road outside her house in Peredelkino, the famous writers' colony south-west of the city. A mutual friend, Alexandra de Lantsheere, had persuaded her to join our party heading out on a weekend wolf hunt near Smolensk and asked us to swing by Peredelkino and pick up Juliet on the way. But it was not in Moscow that we would get to know her well and become great friends. For by late 1994, a year on since Rory had been cut down in the crossfire during the battle for the Ostankino television centre, Juliet's Russian period was drawing to a close; and the most dramatic upheavals of her life – that calamitous tally, the telling of which leaves the hearer awe-struck – were already behind her. In particular, the cancer to which she would succumb twelve years later had already made itself known.

The eye patch that presented itself to our dumb gaze as she slipped quietly into the back of our Ford Fiesta, so visibly signifying the traumatic life of this young mother, twice violently widowed, might also symbolise how fate had pirated her away from the frontline action that she had always sought. Years later, sitting in Juliet's house in Maine on New Year's Eve in 2002, we heard Juliet express that very thought. We reminisced about the tumultuous events that we had all witnessed – the Russian revolution of our own time, which had in part been sparked by that other central episode in Juliet's curriculum of adventure – the defeat of the Red Army in Afghanistan, Juliet lamented her (our) present position – no longer in the thick of the action, but now mere passive spectators of the world's dramas.

As Peshawar and Moscow slipped into the past, the drama of Juliet's life turned in on itself, anchored in her house in the village of Healaugh in the Vale of York, where she brought

The dacha in Peredelkino, Moscow, complete with marble bust of Lenin

up Fynn and Lettice and whence she sallied forth in pursuit
of new projects – including the foundation of the Rory Peck
Trust but also the grind of scraping together some income
from freelance research commissioned by corporate risk
advisory firms. Such work could, at least, slake her innate
wanderlust, with Caribbean destinations offering the right
mix of ambiguous threat lurking in a hot climate. One such
assignment took her back to the cold of Moscow where she
was to garner insight into some murky corner of the Russian
oil business and came to supper for that purpose in our flat
on Maroseyka Street (luckily we managed to rope in for the
evening an Australian friend with the relevant knowledge).

For those who, unlike us, had known Juliet with
Dominique and/or Rory, the Healaugh years may have seemed
outwardly humdrum, her astonishing fortitude redirected now
to withstanding the attrition of the everyday. But just as true
bravery is not fearlessness but rather is forged out of fear,
so true fortitude knows what it is to be broken and, far from
being some kind of magic armour, means picking oneself up
after being crushed. The Juliet whom we met on that drive to
Smolensk seemed a person still overwhelmed, immersed in
silent desolation. We quickly refrained from attempts at chatty
small talk (aided in that matter by having to concentrate on the
roadside traffic cops waving their extortionate wands every
few miles along the road of Napoleon's retreat). As for the
wolf hunt, it richly deserved her disdain, farcical non-event as
it turned out to be; but had she not been so bowed down, she
would have revelled in the absurdity.

A few weeks later we found her more relaxed as we took
her out to dinner with a couple of other friends in the city:
but when the time came to go home, she would not hear of
any of us helping her on her way – and even seemed vexed
by the suggestion. As she headed out alone into the freezing
night to find a gypsy cab to take her back to Peredelkino, we

realised that she was determined to stand on her own two feet as opposed to giving even the faintest impression of being a needy wretch. By Easter Day 1995, when, children and house guests in tow, we went to a lunch party which Juliet gave in Peredelkino, she seemed to have escaped the deep winter of sorrow (though the same could not be said of the actual winter on that bright mid-April day, as our snow-suited toddlers Lettice and Victoria foundered in the deep powder on their search for Easter eggs).

FORTITUDE AND FUN

In later years, the stark contrast between that first Moscow encounter and the Yorkshire-based Juliet whom we would come to know so well, with all her cheerful hospitality and always charming company, impressed upon us the real measure of her fortitude. Juliet herself would occasionally let slip a mention of days of depression – not, of course, in a spirit of self-pity, which she abominated, but rather because she worried about the effect that her inner demons might be having on the children.

Here is a piece of wisdom from Robert E. Lee, one of those generals whose gifts of military command also produced fine moral insight.

Though battle may test the will of men, the sheer constancy of daily life can require as much fortitude as the bloodiest battle. For are not the enemies at your door? Does not the press of time wear heavy on your mind? Have not the decisions of the past come back to haunt you, again and again? Do not your accounts fluctuate with the ebb and flow of daily commerce, rising and falling like the evening tide?

For us, these questions sum up this part of Juliet's achievement after her retreat from Moscow. The obvious 'enemy at the door' was her periodically metastasizing cancer, with Juliet's principal concern always being the children: in the case of the episode discovered in 2000, that meant keeping from them the real reason for her having to go to hospital for an operation. As for being haunted by the past, she would sometimes share what seemed to be a suspicion that her afflictions were some sort of pay-back for things she had done in her earlier life. But such painful flashes of introspection were rare. Although she would tell of her troubles with plain honesty, Juliet was not one for dwelling on them with others. When we went up to Healaugh for New Year's Eve in 2004, she mentioned that she had a sore arm. Needless to say, she made light of it. But at one point, her stoicism was overwhelmed by the pain. We could tell only because she was cut short in mid-sentence – no sound, let alone cry; only silence. A visit to the doctor – but only after we had left – revealed that a growing tumour above her wrist had snapped the bone in her forearm.

Such sombre recollections are unrepresentative of the sunny and carefree times we spent with Juliet. The times in question were escape from routine: brief, hastily arranged, weekends at York Road Mews; or a few days in London to take the children to some West End shows; or – a particular coup for us given the competition with her beloved Maine – Juliet and the children joining us for a while in a house we had rented one summer in the Mugello hills to the north of Florence. All these moments – delightful and frequent as they were (though as far as we were concerned they could never be frequent enough) – leave us unqualified to contribute to a systematic record of Juliet's life in her last years. We no more than brushed against her rich and varied Yorkshire activities: her career in local politics; parish events and causes; her serving on the Yorkshire Ambulance Service Trust; and her hunting.

How we would have loved to have been part of that hunting scene! All it would have taken would have been for us to get our act together on taking up riding again before we eventually did, in 2005 – though that was just in time for some hacks around Healaugh crowded with incident thanks (for example) to Juliet's dodgy tack (a broken girth spotted by Brigitte saving Ishbel Macpherson from a potentially painful mishap) or the determination of Light Brownie, still Russian at heart, to unseat his flailing mount aka Christopher who could only envy Brigitte cantering away on Dazzler, the much-loved giant of a mare – blind in one eye like Juliet.

As things were, it amused Juliet to cast us in the role of urban intellectuals who, during the hunting season, should arrive on a Saturday afternoon, let ourselves into the house and read our books by the fire in that warm, homely drawing room of heavy dark Russian furniture. Juliet's love of beauty was pursued through a taste that was strongly individual but entirely without airs – as, for example, in the slightly beaten-up tea bowls made by the Gardner Imperial Porcelain Factory with the stamp of the imperial double-headed eagle still visible on their base that she had snapped up in Central Asian bazaars; and, provided it was beautiful, bling was also good in her book – not to mention fun, a highlight for her being Brigitte's sporting Chanel kit for riding.

We soon learnt that there was no need to bring books from London, unless it was to add to the pile of new books on the left of the front door. Then there were richly stocked shelves to be browsed, new surprises in every bedroom – not to mention the fine travel library in the downstairs loo. Weekends were not nearly long enough to compare notes on scraps of reading: the pile of Sunday papers generally lay untouched.

In this mode, we could only live the hunt vicariously through the tales told by Juliet and those of her friends like Catherine Cairns and Jonathan Small who shared her passion for the chase and who became our friends. Maximum exposure to hunting talk came during one Saturday-evening guinea fowl feast in the scarlet cocoon of Soviet propaganda posters – offset by the Murano wine glasses and deep blue tumblers – that was Juliet's snug dining room. Fellow guests included an MFH of the Middleton and conversation turned on a different kind of chase: who had made a pass at whom at the Hunt Ball, leading to catalogues of the exploits of those Don Juans of the Yorkshire hunting scene – and, it appeared, many a predatory Doña Juana – that made us feel sheltered metropolitan folk.

Gossip was a mainstay of our chat, with current affairs providing a reliably rich seam for us miners of folly, fraud and humbug in that heyday of New Labour and the moral corrosion of easy money. Juliet relished the discomfiture of the likes of Peter Mandelson, Geoffrey Robinson and Conrad Black. She revelled in the human gallery of weakness and vice, especially when redeemed by individual charm, courage and a noble cause. Her disabused fascination with Afghan mujahideen got a new lease of life after the American military overthrew the Taleban regime in the wake of the '9/11' attacks and she was commissioned to provide a prosopography of those (briefly resurgent) Pushtun and Tajik warlords.

The flaws and foibles of more everyday characters – from the local clergy to the neighbours we would visit for aperitifs before Saturday dinner or Sunday lunch – were likewise placed under amused scrutiny and, as called for, properly deplored. Juliet never affected a saintly benevolence, but neither was there ever any hint of the Pharisaic about her. Her bracing lack of sentimentality could make her seem tough on her children, dogs, horses and, above all, herself (her reaction to a lost dog: 'disappointing'). Love was too important to be flaunted: it just stoked itself at the molten core. At heart, and above all when anything serious might be at stake and even more especially when there was a risk or reality of hurt, Juliet's forbearance and compassion shone out.

LESSONS OF LIFE AND DEATH

Juliet's breezily robust attitude to death had much more to it than mere aversion to sentimentality or even a defensive carapace to help her cope with everything that she had been through. Those elements were certainly present. In 2002, for example, a young British photo-journalist called Roderick Scott was killed in Ingushetia. In the true spirit of Rory and all of his kind, Scott had joined a party of Chechen fighters mounting a raid from their base in a mountain gorge on the Georgian side of the border. As if in a latter-day Tolstoy novella, the raiding party was surrounded and destroyed by Russian special forces who were apparently surprised to find a British passport as they combed through the corpses. We had learnt that Scott's stricken parents had been put in touch with Juliet; but when we asked her about this, she only said, 'been there, done that'. On a lighter note, but one that pointed beyond such cool fatalism, she gave short shrift to the lamentations for Lady Di who, pronounced Juliet, had been 'very lucky' to meet with that fatal road accident in Paris.

On display at moments like these was an unmistakeable religious impulse that embraces our existence and desires to make the best of it – for which facing squarely up to death is a help rather than a hindrance, in fact a necessity. This is the opposite of fatalistic resignation, as could be seen from the spirit in which Juliet founded the Rory Peck Trust. As she used to put it, what differentiated her from most dependants of journalists killed or disabled 'in action' was that she had been able to fall back on family and friends for shelter and support. So she sought to make such practical relief a reality for others less fortunate in the same misfortune. Later, she set herself to systematic study of the root of much of the suffering she had encountered in life by embarking on a PhD thesis in York University's Politics Department on conflict resolution in Iraq and Afghanistan. And she applied to herself that same will to beat back adversity. In the case of the strict vegan diet that helped parry her cancer for half a decade, this produced a symbolic bonus for the world by burnishing her beauty to perfection.

THE ART OF FRIENDSHIP

Good friends delight in learning from each other in free and varied exchanges, often revelling in the exchange as an end in itself with the actual content barely perceptible. When a friend dies young, however, those lessons become a gift distilled by memory. Remembering Juliet has, for us, much to teach about how best to live and die. But we also hold on to the vivid memory of a friendship that was lived in the present. There is a kind of escapism about friendship that certainly applies to us and Juliet. The magic formula requires a measure of shared interest and experience combined with a good dose of otherness. Such friends seek each other's company for refreshing contrast from the daily round. Thus we glanced against Juliet's present and past life with fascination, amusement, awe and edification. Such friendship is not much use for factual biography. But it can provide a mirror for the friends themselves – how they were and, in our case telling this tale, how we are. And this mirror is panoramic. For Juliet's delight in varied and splendid company has left a little platoon whose own shared friendship is something that stems from her and in which her spirit lives.

Picking Up the Pieces
Priscilla Smith (II)

In December 1990, Juliet married Rory Peck. She had
telephoned me a few days before and asked me what I
thought. I had known Rory for years. He and I, along with all
his crazy friends, had had some wild times in Northern Ireland,
and I had been to his wedding to Janey. Juliet had met Rory
through Afghanaid. My heart sank. Marrying Rory was bound
to be dangerous: he smelt of adventure and could resist nothing
that involved risk. But at least this time she had given us some
forewarning. Sadly Julie's normal vicar felt unable to remarry
her, and they were wed in the Catholic church in Peshawar
some ten days later. Almost immediately, the Gulf War broke
out and Rory disappeared to Baghdad to do some fearless
insider filming. This was to set the tone for their years together.

Rory made Julie happy. Much of the pain and heartache
of the previous few years was gradually healed and she was to
be seen smiling and relaxed. She came home more, was more
herself and Rory's two boys Jamie and Ali had fun alongside
Fynn and, subsequently, Lettice.

How Lettice was conceived always baffled me: she
was born nine months after Julie spent several weeks in
the London hospital recovering from a broken back. In
Peshawar, she had been thrown from one of her *buzkashi*
stallions when it had cornered too fast. Some men picked her
up from the track and drove her in a truck back to the house,

where Rory arranged for an air ambulance to fly her back to England. She was bubble wrapped and sedated before being packed into the jet. She described the terrifying sense of being stacked in a small space and kept immobile during the flight. Rory had to pay for the fuel up front – fortunately he had plenty of cash from his war filming money. On arrival in London, the medics expressed how fortunate she was to have avoided paralysis – the nerves were so close to the break that any part of that journey in the truck to the final arrival in the hospital could have done irreparable damage. She lived in the hospital room in the grim area off the London Road for six weeks. She bore the discomfort with characteristic fortitude, but not the nursing staff who never lived up to her exacting standards – although this fury was probably due to the inconvenience of having to lie still for so long.

Rory and Julie went to Ireland, where she recuperated from her injury. They lived in the little cottage at Prehen, and here Hero Lettice Zuleika was born. Rory told the boys that she was found in the cabbage patch. Julie, in true teasing form, told me that they were going to call her Jezebel: all my theological training bristled at such a slander on the poor child! Lettice leapt into life, full of vigour. But soon Rory was absorbed in the uprisings in Moscow and it was not long before they set up home there, in a dacha in the suburbs, where they collected dogs and horses.

Increasingly Julie went to the war zones with Rory, leaving the children with a Russian nanny. Julie reasoned that if Rory was going to dangerous places she wanted to be with him; so frequent trips to Georgia, Sarajevo and Tbilisi ensued. The strain showed on them. Some weeks later, things were hotting up in Moscow. Dare-devil that he was, Rory had climbed into the White House and filmed from sitting at Yeltsin's desk. This time his luck ran out. On 3 October 1993, he was outside the Ostankino TV Tower filming the uprising when Yeltsin's men turned their attention on the journalists: Rory was one of the forty-seven killed in the crossfire. Julie had been with him but had left to look for some equipment. When she returned he was gone. Searching the streets for him through the night revealed nothing and eventually in the early hours of the morning she went to the morgue, where her search ended. It was the telephone call that I had long dreaded – it had only been a matter of how long it would take to happen.

Repatriating a body is a long and difficult business. I was in the early stages of pregnancy, feeling ghastly, and I would not have been much use out in Russia, but her friends were amazing and they swept in. Some days later we went to bury Rory in the family vault at Prehen in Ireland. My parents had gone on ahead and felt ill at ease, cold-shouldered by Carola [Peck, Rory's mother] who in her grief could not reach out to them (she had never accepted Julie as Rory's wife). We arrived to find them sad and isolated, wandering the garden, feeling neither part of the Peck wake nor of those in Juliet and Rory's cottage where they had been told that Juliet needed her friends not her family. It was a difficult day.

The church was packed, the weather was gloomy, the memories flooded around. Julie was brave as ever and buoyed up by her friends' support and the hero's welcome that Rory had been given. She survived the second ordeal that had shattered her life. The world of the journalists closes in on these occasions and real kindness was shown.

We left Julie at Prehen to sort out her belongings and the children. It was not long before she rang me in desperation: life for her there was unbearable. She was struggling with her grief and how to cope with the children and a family traumatised by the death of the oldest son. I booked a crossing on the ferry from Stranraer and belted down that long road to the docks, narrowly catching the boat and arriving fracked and exhausted. Faithful Catherine Cairns was there in the little cottage with

Julie, allowing me time to retire and sleep when the night promised to become a long drinking session. But I did not sleep much, being woken in the early hours by the sound of loud and desperate wailing from the bedroom across the way. Later we discussed our helplessness at the grief that engulfed Juliet, and also the difficulty in reaching out to her, locked as she was in her mental suffering. For me there had been too many years of distance and rebuffed friendship to have the courage physically to sit beside her. All I felt I could do was to wait for the moment when she might let me in. Gradually that was all going to change and it came through her ill health.

It was my aunt Margaret, at Rory's funeral, who noticed that something was wrong with Julie's face. From her description, her husband Jeremy, who was a renowned medic, suspected that Julie had a growth behind her eye. We began a series of doctors' appointments, first in Leeds and then in Manchester, each fast-tracking her to yet higher and higher expertise. It was before one of these hospital visits that my father rang me with words that would give me courage to cope with what was coming: 'You may get bad news today but tell her not to be afraid. God has brought her back to England to save her life.' I know that if my father makes an *ex cathedra* statement I need to take note. As we went from one bit of bad news to the next, these words inspired a sense of peace. Because of my uncle's contacts we were fast-tracked to the top eye surgeon, who happened to be in Manchester, and so Brian Leatherbarrow entered our world.

Mr Leatherbarrow was hardly older than us, earnest, lean, slightly anxious and held in much veneration by all around him. A bevy of medical staff and students in different uniforms buzzed around him, each vying for attention. We were ushered into a room where he examined Julie's scans and carefully and sensitively outlined the seriousness and rarity of a cancer in the lachrymal gland, and the (extremely low) statistics of its occurrence. It was aggressive and needed to be operated on, resulting in the loss of her eye. Looking at her gravely he explained that this situation was normally found in old people and the previous six cases were all at least septuagenarians. The poor man was left quite speechless when she replied, 'Well, I shall reduce your average age considerably then.'

It wasn't the only time that we had fun at the expense of the medics – it was the best way to get through one waiting area after another: the painstaking way in which nurses would explain procedures so as not to hurt Julie's feelings just made us laugh all the more. She was a model of determination and resolution and we saw the funny side of every situation.

But the truth was that it was bleak; her eye would go – the whole of it, right back to the edge of the brain as the tumour was so deep. It would leave a huge gaping cavity which remained a weeping sore for the rest of her life, scabbing over again and again but never healing completely. She was to have titanium implanted which would graft with the bone and enable her to have a prosthetic eye. But it never was to be: the implants did not work, and besides, she reasoned that it was less confusing for people to deal with a patch than to keep wondering which eye was looking at them.

I believe that she treated the situation lightly because she had seen far worse when the war-wounded from Afghanistan were fixed with prosthetic limbs. To her, the loss of an eye seemed minor and at least she had another – and more to the point it was her good one that remained and not the one for which she already had a monocle. The loss of the eye was to cause interest for the rest of her life, from children in the streets pointing to the 'pirate' to the official in the Nigerian Embassy who doubted the authenticity of her patch (her photograph had been taken before the operation) – she removed the patch, his mouth dropped and he asked, 'Did they do that to you in *my* country?' The visa was granted.

After various operations and twelve long weeks of radiotherapy she, sporting her elegant velvet eye patch, was free to pick up the pieces of her life. She had indeed been brought back to England to save her life.

YORKSHIRE

'I can't have that'
Jane Head

Jane's son George and Lettice met on the first day of prep school and have been firm friends ever since. With Juliet travelling often, Lettice spent a lot of time with the Heads, and Jane and Juliet grew close.

The year is 1995. Who is this woman who turns up at school in her crisp white shirt and European jeans? Why do people flock around her all the time? How does she manage to bat them away with the skill and coolness of David Gower? Hum. Note to self: avoid at all costs; clearly not friendly.

It was time to establish contact, so, with my aide memoire rattling around in my head, I made my approach during the school sports day. Juliet was with someone I knew well, so I stood alongside her good eye with a wide smile waiting to be brought into the conversation. However, Juliet continued to hold the gaze of the other person, refusing to acknowledge my existence – embarrassing both for me and the other person. Dismissed without a word, I had been thwarted with masterful skill. Not a great start.

Things did change and when they did, they changed quickly: we became firm and good acquaintances, a foundation to what would become friendship. I realised that much of the 'flocking' was intrigue mixed with a dash of pity. What also became apparent was that Juliet batted away potential new friends simply because she had a plethora of long-term close friends, causes and committees: space in her life was minimal.

Juliet invited George for the first time to holiday with the family in Maine in the summer of 1998. 'Jane.' (Juliet had a habit of saying one's name rather than formally greeting you.) 'We would simply love George to come to Maine with us *but* I must make it understood we are there for three weeks. I cannot make any alteration to plans. Homesickness is not an option.' George was a reserved child and he regarded the invitation with horror. I thought my enthusiasm for the project would overcome any hurdles and that Juliet would never notice.

We met on the day of departure at York station. As we stood on the platform we saw Juliet elegantly glide in with only minutes to spare, not once looking behind her to check if her entourage was still present; they chased behind, desperate

York Road Mews with Blackberry and Vandal (aptly named), two beagles which Juliet temporarily adopted for the hunt

to keep up, pushing hugely over-loaded trolleys – one of which included a cast-iron fire grate. Luggage loaded, we bade a brief farewell to George and the doors closed. Whistle blown, the train slowly edged forward and George burst into tears. Juliet's head spun almost 360 degrees, like a scene from *The Exorcist*. As her piercing stare sped away from me, what could I do other than shrug, smile and wave?

These holidays were to become a regular feature for many years, all of them treasured by George. One summer George's House Master lunched there, after which Juliet sent me a card to tell me that Guy was a splendid man, likening him to Mr Chips as a true educationalist. I shuddered a little on Guy's behalf, wondering how rigorously he must have been interrogated in such a short space of time to acquire this strong and favourable opinion; I imagined Juliet's bad cop, bad cop method, usually employed when time was against her.

Often Juliet's funds were short. But Juliet and I guiltily shared a secret adoration of shoes. Once, Juliet organised a trip – on pennies – to Paris. I received a series of rhetorical texts from Juliet, who was clearly tussling with the devil: 'I'm walking past a window and there is a pair of shoes … I'm going in … I'm trying them on … I'm sitting in a café with a coffee and my new shoes.' I replied that the coffee was an extravagance. On her return, the shoes sat on a chair while the two of us peered at them as one would the Pietà. We agreed that she had definitely done the right thing.

For all the years I knew Juliet, there were only brief pockets of time when she was perfectly well. The prelude to the end came on the way to see the end-of-term play. We had driven up together, chatting all the way, but moments before entering the hall (with precision timing to prevent discourse), Juliet told me that her illness had spread and it would mean she would no longer be able to hunt. 'I *can't* have that,' she said, entering the hall, Juliet's way of telling me that the discussion was over.

The day before Juliet died I drove to her house, but could not bring myself to intrude, instead parking outside in the lane. There was a heavy winter sunset in the distance and some hunters passed the car returning after the day's excitement. I remember wondering if she could hear the horses trotting by. The next day I drove to the house and could see by Catherine Cairns's face as she stood in the garden, talking on the phone, that it was all over.

Juliet had a fire inside her that roared most fiercely when all around her was dark. She dealt in truths, dismissing time wasters and manipulators. Her campaign poster when running for the local council, showing a photo of Juliet with the slogan 'an eye on the future', was a perfect illustration of her self-deprecating wit, honesty and sincerity. Her slow, deliberate speech was a mixture of eloquence and simplicity. Her interest in everything, her fierce independence, her dancing spider-like hand writing, her sharp intellect, her aloofness, her stoicism, her compassion, her sense of justice, the pride and love for her children and her ability to seize each day – all these created the legend that is now Juliet.

'That is *so* irritating'
George Head

George first met Lettice Crawley Peck on a nursery playground. They became fast friends and have remained so ever since.

I should preface this note by saying that although I have been friends with Lettice since 1995, and had much exposure to Mrs Peck, my memories are limited: my timid childhood-self

Juliet with Fynn and Lettice at Craddock Lodge, Devon, Simon and Mary Crawley's house in the late 1990s

found her so formidable that it became my goal to make sure I was where she was not. She always remained Mrs Peck, and never Juliet, despite Lettice's protests – she would say, 'But Mummy, I call Mrs Head "Jane".' (This was not true: Lettice opted for a series of fictional names for my parents – Guinevere, Arthur and some witches from her novel, before settling with Mr and Mrs Head.) But Mrs Peck would joyfully wind Lettice up, cheerfully replying, 'Oh don't worry darling, I'm *sure* "Mrs Peck" is fine.'

I was scolded twice by Mrs Peck.

The first time, I ignored her no-electronics-when-staying-over rule, and brought a Gameboy. Fynn was subsequently busted playing 'Mario' at three a.m.; the offending item was confiscated and returned to my mortified mother. I was let off lightly, receiving only a deadly, silent stare from Mrs Peck – whose attitude to fun was very much 'fields, not phones', or perhaps 'trees, not tech'.

Riding was a huge part of Lettice and Fynn's childhood. Pictured here on Sparky and Melbourne, c. 1997

The second time, Mrs Peck, Lettice, Fynn and I had been into York to buy a non-stick frying pan to hang next to the Le Creuset set. We returned in time for lunch and I was asked to be in charge of bacon and eggs – in the new pan, of course. Very aware that I was no chef, and being about nine at the time, I thought as long as the bacon kept moving, it couldn't possibly burn. I was right, and proudly served my contribution to the table. Mrs Peck went to inspect the new pan, and was horrified to find that her daughter's moronic friend – me – had scored virtually all of the non-stick, from the new, treasured now non-non-stick pan. It's hard to transfer to paper, but imagine a voice of frustration, disappointment, and resentment, when Mrs Peck exclaimed with raised voice, while holding the now-lacerated pan in the air: 'Oh, *George*!' followed by a sharp intake of breath, 'That is *so* irritating.' I have yet to be so efficiently crushed.

Weekends in Healaugh

Ishbel Macpherson (II)

It is Friday evening and I have just fought my way through the horror that is the Tube at rush hour to King's Cross and thrown myself on to the seven p.m. train to York with seconds to spare. I make my way straight to the dining car to be greeted by Maria, the dining car manager, who points me to a table that has a hand-written 'Reserved' sign on it. Beaming up at me from the table are Tim Pope, back from one of his liquid 'lawyers' lunches', Philip Dayer, stressed from another week in the City, and Catherine Cairns, looking fractious. We are the regular gang for the monthly trips to York Road Mews for the weekend. So regular in fact that Maria had given me her mobile phone number so that I could call her up and tell her how many we would be on that trip and she would put a 'Reserved' sign on a table, or tables as necessary, to make sure those pesky first-class diners didn't squeeze us out. She also always got our libations ready too: a bottle of white for Tim; a small beer for Philip; a bottle of red for Catherine; and a bottle of champagne for me, beautifully chilled.

The irregulars included Jonathan Small, Helen Jacobsen, Charles Colville, Brigitte and Christopher Granville and Charlotte Black. We have a rollicking good time on the train, polishing off our personal bottles and making friends with everyone else in the dining car, sometimes to their alarm (never to be forgotten the time when Catherine acted out the whole of the Battle of Rorke's Drift, including the final struggle in that tiny redoubt, made of biscuit tins, to complete strangers). We tumble off the train at York and into a taxi to York Road Mews.

What a merry band we are as we stagger into the house to find a stone cold sober Juliet patiently waiting for us in front of the fire in the overstuffed drawing room. A quick 'tisk', then she sets about the important task of getting us yet more drinks. The world is then sorted out until the wee small hours, or until we fall over, whichever was the sooner, and then off to bed.

This routine lasted for all of the thirteen years or so that Juliet lived in Healaugh, with the occasional shift in personnel. It was marvellous, a haven for us worker bees away from the grind of the big city. We regulars each had our own bedroom, which we defended fiercely, and Juliet made sure that it felt like a real home away from home for us.

Saturdays would be a slow start. Befuddled, we would slowly wend our way into the kitchen to be greeted by the motley pack of dogs Juliet kept. All rescue dogs, all therefore psychologically damaged and none troubled by any form of training. Harry, the terrier, was the longest lasting. He once went walkabout for five years, until he got picked up by the police about eighty miles from home. When Juliet brought him back he just marched into the kitchen, growled at the then occupant of 'his' bed, looked around expectantly for his supper, and then curled up as though nothing had ever happened. We had no idea where he had been for all that time, but he came back better behaved than when he went away. Then there were Sally and Tessa, sleek, graceful greyhounds, Quentin, a pathetically needy Staffie, and the beautiful Finn Barr, a black Labrador who later was stolen just after having been to gundog boarding school.

After some restorative caffeine, it was time for the great outdoors. Walks with the chaotic dogs, or maybe a ride on one of Juliet's wild horses. Like her dogs, her horses were largely untroubled by schooling and had only two gears: stop or very, very fast. One of the most marvellous adrenaline rushes was galloping across stubble fields wondering who was in charge, you or the horse, then deciding that it didn't matter, the most immediate issue being to stop before the next county. My favourite was Dazzle, a huge black mare with only one eye, a relatively late addition to the menagerie. Juliet used to take her hunting, each short of an eye: the mind boggles.

Once the cobwebs were well and truly cleared it was then time to go to a pub for lunch for the statutory plate of chips with something (it didn't really matter what).

Sometimes after lunch we would go on an outing, Castle Howard or the site of the Battle of Towton or the York & Ainsty point to point. Sometimes we just mooched around, popping to the supermarket to stock up on provisions (principally booze). Cooking supper was a collective exercise, and often

Lunch in the garden at York Road Mews c. 2003. L to R: Philip Dayer, Ishbel Macpherson, Tim Pope, Letty, Izzy Phillips, Charlotte Black

an argumentative one as different culinary philosophies clashed. Catherine and Charlotte were often at it hammer and tongs; I acted as chopper and peeler; Philip would duck; Tim would go through the fridge throwing things out if they were mouldy; and Jonathan would go for a bath.

Supper was in the small dining room, painted red, dominated by a huge stone bust of Lenin, with Stalinist posters glaring at us angrily from the walls. The round table, covered in a fading, fraying Afghan cloth, was set with the 'good' china, silver cutlery and those gloriously lovely – but terrifying – Venetian gold-topped wine glasses.

Sometimes a guest or two, sometimes not, but always delicious food, no matter how chaotically produced, lashings of drink and stimulating conversation between good friends. Politics and hunting featured large. Juliet had an amazing knowledgeable world view and cared passionately about those less fortunate; more than once we turned up to find that she was housing a homeless person, or Eid the asylum seeker, for a few days. She gave practical help were she could, held no truck with any superior airs and hated anything to do with the European Union. A die-hard Tory, she believed in good manners, valued tradition, freedom of the individual from interference from the state and equality of opportunity for all. To her, the greatest sin was to be dull or defeatist. She would argue her point of view furiously and eloquently, often flooring her equally outspoken guests comprehensively. After clearing up the debris of dinner, without any stacking at table – another terrible sin – the party would move to the drawing room to continue the debate.

The drawing room was dark green and crammed with over-sized furniture collected from her travels around the world, and every surface was covered with interesting bits and photographs. There were photographs of Dominique, Rory, the children, animals and Juliet in a bikini. A Russian painting of the storming of the Winter Palace took up most of the wall behind the sofa and, opposite, a large gilt mirror over the fireplace was stacked with invitations. It was a housewife's nightmare, which is why Juliet chose not to bother. She felt life was too interesting to spend time on the mundane; anyway, a little dirt never hurt anybody. The dust was legendary: an over-enthusiastic flop on to a sofa would send clouds of the stuff up, along with the dog hair. We even found a dead mouse in the toaster once. It was all so classic Juliet: eclectic, even a bit exotic, eccentric and anything but dull.

Once again we would all stay up too late, roaring delightedly at each other before repairing to our usually freezing cold bedrooms (thank goodness for her large collection of electric blankets).

Sunday would start gently, a trip to church in the next-door village for those who so chose, or more fresh air until it was time to draw up the battle lines for the communal making of Sunday lunch. Particularly contentious for our Sunday roast was the making of the gravy, but bread sauce often turned out to be surprisingly problematic too. We squabbled happily, tripped over dogs, peeled, stirred and chopped our way into a traditional feast which we ate with relish, all the while dissecting the previous evening's guests, if any, or the main stories in the papers.

Ishbel Macpherson, Ali, Fynn, unknown, Catherine Cairns

Then it was time to leave. We reluctantly packed our way off to the station and on to what was invariably an overcrowded train back to London. We would sit disconsolately, often not speaking, sad that yet another glorious weekend was over. We were usually exhausted, too, from so much merrymaking.

We made sure that we never left without having set the date for the next trip.

Over the Yorkshire years Juliet was ill from time to time, struggled for money most of the time, and quite often was lonely – yet none of this ever cast a shadow over the joy of those weekends. Juliet created an environment where all who visited felt the warmth of good company, the thrill of stimulating conversation and just had sheer fun.

Fynn and Letty tolerated us too, when they were at home. Fynn usually politely patient and Letty usually in the middle of the room saying, 'Look what I have learnt at school this week, no, really, look at me.' She was never going to be a shrinking violet, was she?

Faith in Life
Frank Houghton Brown

Frank was the huntsman of the Middleton hounds, in Yorkshire, for fourteen seasons, and met Juliet there.

I rarely paid any attention to who was hunting in the field but Juliet was not the kind of person to go unnoticed: not that she pushed herself to the fore, but her eye patch and slightly haughty demeanour with her distinctive laugh and plummy voice were unmistakeable. It turned out that Juliet's father had been the vicar in the village of Culworth in Oxfordshire, where I was brought up.

Catherine Cairns was like a double act with Juliet and the pair of them had so much energy and vitality, like a couple of new religious converts to the cause, eager to take in and soak up as much of the hunting as they could, in all its forms. Juliet made huge

Juliet hosted an annual hunt meet at York Road Mews. With Jackie Gillam and Walter Wharton

efforts to involve me in the comings and goings of York Road Mews and I was always enthusiastic to go anywhere for a meal, not that her food was particularly appetising: nearly always rather anaemic-looking chicken, usually cooked with copious quantities of lemon and not available until nearly midnight. There was however much learned and erudite conversation to which I listened attentively like a fly on the wall, eager to soak up some of the intoxicating talk of travel to far-flung places and high-minded politics, in the hope that it might somehow rub off on my own insular little bubble of Yorkshireness. Juliet puffed away in a rather affected manner at her café crème cigarillos and the smoky sitting room was made bearable by copious amounts of wine; I stared in wonder at the fantastic tapestry overhanging the fireplace in its bohemian splendour. It seemed like there was always a host of intelligentsia staying, arriving from a late train or leaving at a strange hour. I was just an interested observer.

Healaugh 2002. Juliet was a staunch supporter of the Countryside Alliance's battle against the fox-hunting ban

I remember Juliet asking me to come with her to Sunday lunch with her sister's family, the Smiths, and turning up rather scruffily dressed without having given it any thought at all. I was mortally embarrassed to find that a tweed suit and shiny brogues were the order of the day and Juliet thought it was hysterically funny.

It was Juliet's remarkable candour and individuality that I found so magnetic. She was the first person who seemed to know about everything; worldly to the extreme, but to whom you could ask any question and not be pooh-poohed for your naïve ignorance. Her complete outward immunity to her own suffering was also totally incredible to me. Never had I come across someone who had such faith in life: such an ability to turn the spotlight away from themselves in the most selfless and stoic fashion but with such humility that it was not an issue. I still now look to Juliet for strength and hope that I may be blessed with a tiny fraction of the strength she had.

Frustrations of Local Politics
Brian Percival

Juliet and Brian knew each other through local politics. In 1999, they both were elected to Selby District Council, Juliet representing the Bilbrough and Brian the Appleton Roebuck wards.

Juliet was my friend, my confidante, my irregular drinking partner and my political soul-sharer.

When Juliet and I were elected, the Tories were in opposition and somewhat in disarray. Neither of us had had any real experience of being in a party that had no power. We spent the first two years getting to know the ropes and the pointlessness of opposition politics.

We both served on the planning committee. We were determined that what we thought were hitherto irrational decisions and ill-thought-through consents should be stopped – little knowing that we were still in the era (thankfully now past) when the majority party influenced officers' reports and recommendations. At times, it was very frustrating.

She lived in Healaugh and I had my offices close by in Tadcaster. After a bad session, I would call round to her home, with its decor reflecting her earlier life spent in what was then the USSR. I would consume brandy from her well-stocked drinks trolley, we would discuss the state of the District and the country, and what ought to be done and what could not. I would then drive indirectly home through the little-used back roads.

Juliet came with the baggage of being connected to the Samuel Smith brewing family. Her sister was and still is married into the brewers and Juliet's brother-in-law's brother was a substantial thorn in the side of the District Council. As a result, on the one hand she was treated as a probable conduit of secrets from the Council to the brewery offices, and on the other, hopefully, as a conduit or even a tool in negotiation between the two warring factions. Despite this, she was a councillor of utmost integrity, never taking either role; more probably she was just as out of the loop between the Council and the brewery as anyone. I remember that she once asked the District's CEO how much the brewery had cost the Council in litigation fees. She was told, but kept the information to herself; the brewery would have known the costs in any event.

As a councillor she spoke whenever she thought it was appropriate, both in Council and at party meetings. She was intolerant of fools and ill-thought-through motions that Labour and even some of our own were prepared to offer. But she, like myself, soon recognised that for all the strength and quality of argument, when you are in opposition it counts for nothing. We played politics, we called for named votes, but to no avail: once the Labour executive had made up its mind at their pre-meeting then nothing would change their minds.

After four years, her ward – considered too small – was merged with my own and her tenure of public office was cut short. It did leave me with a hefty majority: only eighty-seven people voted against the former Peck/Percival combined ward.

She was a great campaigner at election times, knocking on doors, asking people to vote Tory, delivering endless election pamphlets that in the main went straight into the bin. With her black eye patch and big floppy hat she was a person that people remembered, and remembered that the Conservatives had sought their vote.

After our four years in opposition the Tories went into the next election with the call for 'Time for Change' and won. The sad thing is that Juliet was not present.

My Father's Watch
Jamie Peck

Jamie is Rory Peck's eldest son from his first marriage to Jane Alexander, from Caledon, Northern Ireland. He currently works for a head-hunting firm in Geneva.

After our father's death, my mother and Juliet tried their best to share holidays between the two families in order to keep the bonds alive. However, being that bit older than my siblings I quickly abandoned family time for trips with friends and weekends in London. As a young teenager I thought there was nothing so tedious as having to spend time with my brothers, sisters and – even more so – parents. I was far more interested in what parties were planned during term breaks and life in Ireland to even contemplate visiting Juliet in Yorkshire. Selfish I know. Today I can look back and say that I should have spent more time with them – but hindsight is a glorious thing.

Losing our father was terrible and the aftermath just as bad: families fight for the memory and reminders of their loved one. This was at least the case in our family, which made it so important to cling on to the good memories and hold on to the precious keepsakes that reminded us of him. Since my father died in Russia while together with Juliet, she held most of his personal effects. These were the things that he would use, love and cherish every day. Value has no importance when it comes to these items, a simple loved jumper was enough. While we could always see them in Yorkshire – and I realise that it's only normal that she would hold them – I could not help but wish to have some part of him for my own.

Life continued and I saw less and less of Juliet, continuing to carve my own path. After boarding school I was invited to apply to the Irish Guards: I refused; I was recommended to apply to university: I refused, choosing instead to start working. In 2003 I had an offer to work in Afghanistan managing a guesthouse, the Gandamack Lodge. I spent my twenty-first birthday in Kabul, not expecting much fanfare or many gifts, yet I received a silk carpet ordered by Juliet and delivered by the shopkeeper. This was the first form of communication we had had for many years. Perhaps in my going to Afghanistan I had risen in her esteem. No matter the reason, this act had reopened interaction between us.

Afghanistan matured me, I understood my father better, I understood the love Juliet and he had for the oppressed parts of the world, and I understood that I needed to be closer to my family. During this time I had applied to university and been accepted. With this date in mind, I left Afghanistan. Waiting for me at home on my return was a small parcel from Juliet. Enclosed was my father's watch. This is the greatest gift I have ever received: knowing that my father wore it, admired it and loved it means the world to me. Such a personal possession that reminds me of him every time I look at it is priceless. However, now every time I do so, I think not only of him, but also of Juliet and will do so for the rest of my life. The kindness and generosity she showed me in giving away his watch will stay with me for ever.

You Haven't Really Travelled Until…

Spencer Crawley

Spencer is the son of Harriet Crawley, Juliet's first cousin. He is now helping set up a venture capital fund investing in technology start-ups.

Juliet was as well travelled as anyone I knew. With this in mind, and being a tiresomely competitive teenager, I always took pleasure in identifying any countries that I had been to that she had not. In time, a tradition began between us. Every time we visited a new country, we would send the other a postcard. This reached its most satisfying moment for me, when, after a European road trip with my mother, I wrote a postcard from sleepy Andorra and sent it off to York Road Mews. Juliet, it turned out, had never been to Andorra. In the subsequent years, I would get postcards from far-flung corners of the earth, signed off with a gloating 'lots of love' in scarcely legible handwriting. No matter where they came from, be it Central Africa, Pakistan or Costa Rica, I could always quietly remind her when we next saw each other, 'Well, you haven't really travelled of course until you've been to Andorra,' to which she would invariably let out a loud laugh.

A Creative Response to Tragedy
Tina Carr

Juliet set up the Rory Peck Trust in 1995. Two years later Tina joined and now she directs the organisation.

One of the best things about being involved in the Rory Peck Trust has been the number of extraordinary, strong women I've been lucky enough to meet. Juliet Crawley Peck was perhaps the strongest and most extraordinary of all – and I was simply terrified of her. Well, perhaps not of Juliet herself, but of the precious heritage with which I felt I'd been entrusted.

In 1997, I was working as a writer and, as writers tend to do, going ever so slightly nuts with the solitude of it all. I was looking for structure, sociability, and an excuse to get away from my desk. A part-time job at a small media charity in Paddington (as it was advertised) seemed the perfect solution. One day soon after I joined, I was sitting on an orange box at the one computer, with my feet propped up on files, when a slim, elegant fairy in a mini-dress and an eye patch appeared in the doorway. 'Hello, I'm Juliet – lunch?'

Off we went to the local Persian café. Juliet was friendly, she had style and a wonderful sense of irony – and she was totally unfathomable. I was a little bit in awe of her so I stayed on safe territory – some girly chat about clothes, friends in common, a bit of gossip, a lot of mint tea. Juliet then began talking about how she started the Trust. And suddenly it shone through – this was driving her. She cared.

We didn't meet that often, but spoke on the phone a lot and I counted greatly on her support and advice – and Juliet gave very good advice.

I think that Juliet's creative response to tragedy led to one of her greatest achievements. She bounced back from events that would have destroyed most people, brought up her children, carried on with her life – and had the idea of starting something that is now bigger and more important than she could ever have imagined.

In 1997, the Rory Peck Trust felt like a sacred cow – and I didn't dare to change anything for a very long time. However over the years, it became clear that if the Trust was to survive and achieve what Juliet wanted – to be a viable source of support to freelancers and their families world-wide – it would have to develop in line with the changing lives and conditions of those freelancers. So change came – and the Trust has prospered. However, at its heart is something that has never changed – the mission and belief that was Juliet's. And I truly believe that this mission has enabled the Trust to survive until today.

Would Juliet have approved? Honestly – I have no idea. But I'm absolutely certain that if I was ever able to meet her again, I would still be in awe.

Julie's Laugh
Nick Crawley

*Nick is Juliet's eldest brother. He is an Anglican clergyman in
the diocese of Bristol.*

When I think of Julie, perhaps the most extraordinary and
exceptional person I have ever known, I remember her
laughing.

I had stayed overnight at York Road Mews. We had had
breakfast and we both needed to go. I put my bag in the car
and was standing at the driver's door. She came up to the
car and, in that unexpected and disarming way, looked at me
with her hand resting above the opposite door. As her face
lit up in a bright smile, she lifted her shoulders and laughed
brightly, freely and carelessly.

Her face suddenly transformed into carefree delight. Her
eyes burst with light and life in a single untethered moment. It
was a moment when life stopped, a moment when our spirits
touched. It was a moment when all the damage of the past was
no more, a moment of forgiveness (for we had hurt each other
in earlier years). In an instant all was repaired, the future open
before us. She had suffered life so deeply and yet was not
chained by these memories: this instant showed it.

Her laugh was strong, assertive, full of humour and
courage, and peaceful and free; it had within it the power to
free others – I know this because it freed me. We could look

forward together, be at one despite the past misunderstandings of Peshawar and London and other times. It seemed that all our humanity touched in that moment of unity.

All her extraordinary attributes were caught up in that moment – her courage to face danger (for even then the cancer was gripping her); her ability to ride and surmount grief and to be a friend and to befriend (many); her determination to live the untethered, wild life of the nobility as previous generations had done; her gritty love of adventure.

Her laugh was so powerful, so winning, so completely disarming: you were welcomed, accepted, lifted and set up. Her voice, with its intonation of forgiveness and excitement, had a power of life to bond you and to raise you up.

And as she laughed and both our lives seemed caught in that moment, I chose then and there to remember for ever that instant as my memory of this wonderful, extraordinary woman that I was so privileged to have as my sister.

A Lucky Impulse Buy

Mark Atkinson

Mark kept various horses at livery for Juliet. He was a master of the York & Ainsty (South) for two seasons and field master for twenty. He now runs 'Atkinson Action Horses', which trains horses for equestrian displays and the screen.

One morning I received a call from Juliet. She said that she had just enjoyed herself at a party somewhere in Scotland until the early hours of the morning, and after several glasses of wine had bought (without seeing or trying) a hunter. I was surprised because Juliet had three horses already. However, she was told this horse was an amazing jumper with the manners of an angel. We talked at length. I felt slightly concerned, as I realised a substantial amount of money had changed hands. Juliet was not, as the horse had come highly recommended by the friend she had met the evening before.

It was arranged for the horse, Max, to be delivered immediately. Unfortunately, Juliet had to go to work in Chile. So I would assess him and she would look forward to hunting him on her return. Juliet had ridden the horse on one occasion whilst still in Scotland and liked him, so all was well.

Max arrived. He was a 16' 3 hands, 3/4 warmblood, 1/4 thoroughbred, a dark bay with a white star; he was a splendid beast – a very kind horse with good paces and a huge, careful jump.

When Juliet returned home, we organised her first day's hunting on Max. We travelled four horses that day. As the second horse was being led off the horse box, Juliet exclaimed, 'Mark, one day I would love to own a horse like that,' pointing to the big bay horse. I said, 'Well that's good, because he is your horse.' The delighted smile followed by a roar of laughter from Juliet is something I will never forget. Though I wouldn't recommend buying a horse unseen at a party, on this occasion it paid off.

Juliet and Max had many happy and exciting days' hunting. For the first time Juliet could cross any country and jump the bigger fences. He was never patient, but he was a tremendous galloper with a very soft mouth – and so perfect for a lady. He also seemed to be able to stay out all day without tiring; all in all a real athlete.

On one occasion Juliet finished hunting early and decided to take a short cut home. This involved jumping several large

Juliet, riding Funny Girl, out with Mark Atkinson and the Middleton Hunt

post and rail fences. Unfortunately, Max put in an almighty leap whilst negotiating one of the fences and Juliet fell off. She was about half a mile from the lorry, not injured but alone and very cross! Max, however, galloped off and we had to send out a search party to find him. He was found by Frank Houghton Brown who took him back to the hunt kennels at Birdsall. He had to stay there for a while until he was well enough to travel as he had been hit by a large cattle feed lorry and had some major injuries. He did make a full recovery and returned to hunting in the field the following season, the only effect being he was now very suspicious of large lorries.

Feminism? 'Pah!'
Jamie Scott

In 1980, Jamie and Rory Peck were in the same platoon at Sandhurst. He is godfather to Rory's eldest son, and first met Juliet in 1993 at Rory's funeral at Prehen.

Rory didn't end up taking the Queen's shilling – he decided at the very end of our course that he was only interested in the romantic side of soldiering. It was only the 'seat of your pants' excitement in fast-moving and far-off lands that seemed to make Rory most happy, not the traditional, mostly mundane and controlled life of a soldier. He married Janey Alexander shortly after leaving Sandhurst. Their divergent lifestyles proved too much to bear for both, as desirous as they were to make each other and their two boys happy.

In 1991, four years after the divorce, Juliet was for Rory the perfect match: two halves of the same coin. Both were most alive when in unconventional, colourful and dangerous environments. I believe the gloss and romance of this world was wearing thin, and it dawned on them that treachery and venal deception were becoming the only players in town. But then the fatal blow struck Rory.

Juliet's move to rural Yorkshire gave her the stability they both had recently wanted for their young family and that she now, after that disaster, so needed. In straitened circumstances and lingeringly ill, with her characteristic but painfully earned stoicism, she drove on her new life, very grateful to her legion of friends, relations and admirers.

Barely did she breathe a word of her losses. It would have galled most people to see those ruffians she had known, filmed, reported on and lived around reap huge rewards with desperate dishonesty in comparison to her honest toils. Her simple moral compass, one of understanding the complexities of human nature rather than right or wrong, led her just to shrug it off. The privilege of hearing her exciting stories – so physically and mentally challenging, but never shown as that – was a rare one.

Some might view her as a deserving beacon of feminism. A deserving beacon most certainly, but I dread to think of the withering look one would have got if 'feminism' – or any '-ism' for that matter – was bandied about. She was as frustrated by ignorance, cant, crass stupidity and lack of achievement in either sex.

Rough scrapes and exciting times on her extensive travels, whether in Pakistan, Afghanistan, Russia or Rwanda, made her fit the mould of those remarkable open-minded and intrepid wanderers on a mission such as Fitzroy Maclean, Paddy Leigh Fermor, Hester Stanhope and Freya Stark. What riveting, fascinating and inspiring books would have roared off the shelves if time had allowed her to write one or two.

I was mesmerised by her vivacity; despite her devastating situation, she – remarkably – continued in her own, uncomplaining way. It was as if the disasters she had suffered reinforced her steeliness. Maybe she was made more aware of the pitfalls of people's personalities and as a result was well suited to her various jobs of finding out accurate and balanced information. I am told her written comments on the main players in Afghan politics are much referred to by relevant 'office wallahs' and have had considerable impact on our government's policy in that region.

She was never one to give away opinions or information lightly. One had to dig hard to discover anything, and no doubt we all wish we had dug a great deal harder. I remember once ringing her mobile to arrange some trivial horse-related matters to get a very odd ring tone on the other end, and, when she answered, it sounded like she was in an aviary. She merely said she was in some very remote place in Indonesia sitting in the jungle looking into some industrial issues!

We were brought closer through our mutual love of horses. Her dogged tenacity was well displayed on the hunting field. Never one for only the social whirl of the day, she was really there for the action up at the sharp end. Riding as hard as the best, fearlessly attempting every obstacle, she was only limited by her finances and the need to retrieve children from school. It appeared to me that she rode as if she had a spare neck in her pocket. Perhaps that exemplified all her doings. Horses loved her gusto and were convinced by her

Juliet's horses, 2003. L to R: Max, Funny Girl, Roo, Dazzler, Light Brownie

kind hands and strong heart to produce their best, and were doubly respectful when they realised they only had three eyes between them and in one case only two.

On the only occasion I persuaded her to come to Scotland to have a day with my local pack, she had found out more about the characters in the field and their history in a very short time than I had in many a year, and somehow it never stopped her being at the front amongst the action all day.

She had such a varied mix of friends, all fascinating. Her conversation was never dogmatic or opinionated, but she questioned with a sensitive fever – yet she rarely mentioned how much she knew or those she had met.

One entertaining weekend at York Road Mews, I remember meeting an elegant and delightful Nigerian that she had met on her travels. He came from a recently deposed and decimated ancient ruling family whose oil-rich lands had been stolen after a military coup. I gathered from others he had many deeds of derring-do to his name and that his group's activities had become quite a *cause célèbre* in the anti-military-coup world. Sadly the coup was savage; I do hope he is still thriving. His delightful calm, quick wit and charm were inspiring. He was rather a typical example of the range of her friends. From businessmen, freedom fighters and journalists, to hunting folk, politicos and writers, her reach seemed endless. And she brought it all together so effortlessly and seamlessly.

Her illness took a beastly long time, yet it never seemed to get in her way; she was always more concerned with the well-being of her family, friends or important matters. It would have given the rest of us a chance to catch up with her, but decrepit old age would have frustrated her furiously.

She was gathered too damn early.

Pranks and Polling
Sue Wrigley

In the mid-1990s, Sue was Chairman of the Selby Constituency Conservative Party. She was looking for possible District Council candidates, and with a view to this, Charlotte Bromet introduced her to Juliet.

I turned up at Charlotte Bromet's house an hour and a half late to find two boot-faced ladies looking at their watches. Juliet suggested that she went immediately as she had other commitments. I persuaded her to stay, although she really did not relish the idea of sitting on the District Council. In the end, Juliet did agree to stand.

Over the next few weeks, I spent a lot of time walking village streets asking people to vote for Juliet. We must have looked a very odd pair, she in green wellies and me in a pair of Gucci loafers – about which she pulled me up. It was all good fun, and we always ended up in a pub (her capacity to drink outstripped mine). Much to my annoyance, Juliet announced that she was going to America for four weeks, leaving two weeks to put out a leaflet and sort out all the minutiae of her election campaign. As her agent, it was a real pain. I read her election manifesto with some relief until I got to the last pledge: be nice to dogs and cats.

We became very good friends. Despite all her problems, she was huge fun, had a wicked sense of humour and was a staunch friend. She had a magnetic personality and took rather boring people like myself into an exotic world, inhabited by spies and elaborate pranks. One April Fools' Day, she got a friend to ask Charlotte Black, who spent time working in Conservative Central Office, to be interviewed by one of the right-wing magazines. Charlotte was absolutely thrilled, and, having told CCO, set up press photo opportunities. Juliet phoned her an hour before the meeting to tell her she was an April Fool: you can imagine how Charlotte reacted. Her second target of the day was the two Smith brothers, who were extremely conservative about planning issues. She put up a planning application poster for high-density residential use on the adjacent land to Oliver Smith's house. By the time she saw them at the Tadcaster brewery, they were having a crisis meeting.

During the first year that Juliet was in Yorkshire, she lived in her sister's house in Healaugh. She told me that she found this very difficult: she found her sister's faith problematic, and she had been at odds with her family for some time. This was, perhaps, down to her more liberal attitude, an attitude she had acquired from her jobs in Afghanistan and Pakistan. She eventually moved into a farmhouse in the same village which her brothers-in-law provided, giving her her own space and the freedom that she missed.

I always felt that I disappointed her in not introducing her to more of my Yorkshire-based friends – but I thought she would find them boring. I never fully understood what Juliet actually did for a job. She alluded to working for an intelligence company that was largely run by ex-MI5/MI6 agents. On one occasion Juliet suggested that I accompany her to the West Indies, where she was working. During this trip, I barely saw her as she was doing something relating to Third World exploitation by major corporations – although we did manage to drink large quantities of rum and try out some very good restaurants.

Juliet was very worried about money. At the time, I was chairman of the North Yorkshire Health Authority. I suggested to her that she might apply for a non-executive post with the Yorkshire Ambulance Trust, as it carried a small salary. Juliet was a mixed blessing to interview, as she could come across as arrogant. Afterwards, she told me that she received a letter from the trust saying that she was unsuitable for the job. Without her consent, I wrote to them to say that she was disabled and a lone mother with two children. When she discovered this, I thought she was going to kill me. However she did get the job – for which she never thanked me.

Juliet's attitude to finance was extremely elastic. Rory had left her with very little money and quite a lot of debt. She was also trying to put both her children through public school. She frequently was unable to pay the fees, and I and others did so for her. She almost expected financial help – although none of us, I am sure, objected. I remember once, whilst listening to her tales of woe in the living room, several children burst in dressed up in Juliet's clothes – which included a Chanel suit and Louis Vuitton accessories.

One day Juliet invited me out to lunch and halfway through announced, in a giggling voice (which always meant trouble), that her cancer had returned. In the following months, I helped as much as I was able. I was with her when the oncologist told her that she only had a thirty per cent chance of getting through the illness if she had chemotherapy, but a very slim chance otherwise. She was determined not to have the chemotherapy. I tried to blackmail her through her duty to her children, but, alas, I failed: she said to me, 'How about you having it for me?' Instead, she took alternative remedies offered by the internet. She did have the colostomy operation, from which she recovered quite well – after about a week, she was out hunting.

SPOOKS AND ADVENTURES

'A bloody good spook'
Christopher James

In 1975, after eight years in the Welsh Guards and the SAS, Christopher joined SIS. He left in 1995, to set up Hakluyt & Company, a strategic intelligence firm.

Marita [Crawley] said that Juliet didn't know what to do, hadn't got any money, liked the idea of Hakluyt and that she'd be jolly good. And she was right. Once we got through the barriers, we hit it off more or less straight away.

We first met in a bar. She was sitting on a stool, had quite a tight skirt on and was dressed to kill – almost dressed to provoke or to put you off. But curiously, she was not showy because as the conversation developed, she was almost apologising for it. There was no bombast. She was rather like an exotic flower: underneath her striking, even intimidating, appearance, there was someone enormously intriguing who didn't want to come to the fore – she was a contradiction in terms.

She had more balls than anyone else I'd ever met. She was slightly shy to start with, not revealing all because she'd been hurt along the line, but there was an inner dynamism that I liked immediately. She was wild as a cat-snake – up for anything and a natural rebel. I can quite easily see her beguiling people through her genuine curiosity. She would have had a brilliant career in MI6. She wouldn't have got in – she was too obviously ballsy and stunning.

I couldn't quite marry her wanting to do this with her reading art or some such and going to work for a Christian charity in India. Perhaps it was something to do with getting some sort of approval from her father; but she also wanted to find out about the world – or life.

A girl like that turns up with a patch on her eye, more or less saying I'll do anything. She had presence. I did think, is this woman mad? I asked her once if she'd do something in Russia and she said she'd find it very difficult to go back. I wondered whether it was to do with Rory. It was the only thing she ever objected to.

Her mind was instinctive rather than intellectual: it was 'let's cut the crap and let's get through to what matters' – decisive and spontaneous. It made her superb at her job and she turned out to be a bloody good spook. I was a spook for twenty-something years and my failings are many, but my dealings with people and getting the best out of them is not one of them. She was a natural, whether it was talking to some ghastly creature under the bridges outside King's Cross or getting arrested in the Niger Delta in pursuit of something we were doing.

I'd describe Hakluyt to would-be clients as a spider's web, with us at the centre and people like Juliet travelling, researching and reporting back. We liked not to rely totally on one person and to have three or four people reporting in – unlike MI6, which goes by and large for single-source reporting which can at times be subjective and inaccurate. We had time to be more analytical. A firm would ask us to go into Russia, for example, to find out what the agenda was or who was working against them. I'd say, what we'll tell you is just what we get from our people reporting in – Juliet or whoever – and we will distil that down and give you our conclusions. It may not be information that you want to hear, but it will help you get a proper assessment of what's going on.

I started from nothing, and used my contacts in business. My last job in 'The Office', as I call it, was being in charge of keeping in contact with major British companies and institutions and giving them information that was relevant to what they were doing. The stuff was, quite frankly, less interesting than what you get from the *Economist* intelligence unit. I wouldn't have paid for it (which of course they weren't). I went round to the Managing Director of Royal Dutch Shell, the biggest oil company in the world at the time, and while he was ploughing through pages of this stuff, I asked if it was of any real interest. He said, 'interesting background, but, frankly, not much use'. The light bulb went on and I asked if it would be useful to have targeted information – to have your own intelligence service – so that instead of fifty intelligence reports, you'd have one. He thought it sounded interesting, and although cautious, indicated the kinds of things that he would be interested in if he were ever to use us.

I kept in touch with him because I liked him; and I was also rather dazzled by talking to the MD of one of the biggest companies in the world. It was new to me; I was living in this schizophrenic world where you were one thing to the outside world, and inside you were meeting people in strange places or doing odd things. So to go into the world of mega business to see people whom you would occasionally read about in the business section of the *Financial Times* ...

This was all talked about in a couple of meetings in 1994. I put Hakluyt together and got Mike Reynolds to join as well as Jeremy Connell. I left 'The Office' in January 1995 and got an office in Welbeck Way. George Jellicoe and Fitzroy Maclean – we were great friends – gave me the impetus to do it. It was wonderful and romantic, and it was fun pulling things together.

In late 1995, the telephone rang and Shell's MD said that he'd got something he'd like to discuss with me. I went to see him and his head of exploration. Greenpeace was orchestrating a campaign against Shell and was disrupting operations in the Niger Delta. The head of the Ogoni tribe had been imprisoned and shot by the Nigerian government and Shell was being blamed. Greenpeace also occupied Brent Spar, a Shell-owned oilrig in the North Sea, to prevent it being scrapped in the North Atlantic.

He said they were worried that it was going to turn even more violent and that they were trying to find out what it was that Greenpeace were up to and what they wanted. Shell wasn't guilty of anything, but it was affecting business hugely and they were happy to come to a settlement. There was a Baader-Meinhof-like group who had infiltrated Greenpeace and was trying to make it much more extreme. Shell was now seen as the unacceptable voice of capitalism, and they needed to counter this. It was affecting Shell's business, its reputation, everything, particularly in Nigeria. He asked if we could do it, and I said we would see what we could do. I thought, 'Fuck, okay.'

Mike Reynolds had one or two very good sources from the Germans because he had served there. But that wasn't enough. So I suggested to Juliet that this might be something that would do. She leapt at it. So this white girl with a patch infiltrated the very heart of Greenpeace, which was – they thought – super, super secure and found out what their agenda was. It took her about nine months of sitting up talking with them, going on courses, becoming more Greenpeace than they were. She went all over the place, and climbed up the hierarchy to become the secretary of an inner group. To me that was the moment when Hakluyt proved itself, thanks to her.

Talking of her determination and her love of adventure, she'd say I've got to go out again – we were being paid quite a lot by Shell to do it – so she would go out. After the tribal leader's death, she went out to Ogoniland. She got arrested – I can't remember why – by the Nigerians. She did say that she had a bit of a rough time, but was released quite soon. I did think, 'Shit, a white woman in a black jail …'

Shell was going to have its AGM simultaneously in London and in Amsterdam or The Hague. The MD said that they were in for a rough ride and didn't want the meeting disrupted – Greenpeace had made sure that one or two of its members had shares so that they could ask embarrassing questions. Juliet went to a Greenpeace meeting in King's Cross or Euston where they were planning what to ask at the AGMs the following day. I got this message from her saying that she'd got all the questions that Greenpeace were going to ask. I took a room at Boodles and arranged to meet Mike Reynolds and Juliet, who was coming straight from the meeting, there. We met her at about half past eleven, got her in through the back door, debriefed her, and she gave us chapter and verse.

Next morning, we got it to the MD who told his board they'd got the entire agenda. He was cock-a-hoop. It was our first huge breakthrough. It saved them tens if not hundreds of millions of pounds because they were able to deflect the questions. To have the agenda of the people who were going to disrupt the biggest company in the world's AGM was fucking brilliant. It was the biggest coup anybody could ask for. It all blew up in the end and there was a lot of coverage, but Juliet's role never appeared.

I thought she was fabulous – fun, and exotic. She was a genuine, genuine friend and although I make friends fairly easily on the surface I'm really committed to people who are different and have got balls, which she had. We would sit up and talk for hours. She told me about being arrested in Rwanda. She was roughed up, she said, by this cocky young officer throwing his weight around, and talked her way out of it. He asked what she was wearing the patch for, so she lifted it and showed him to prove the point. Apparently he virtually collapsed, thinking she was a witch.

She thrived on these sorts of situations and took on another persona, becoming steel. She wasn't foxed or fazed by anything; I would have put her in for a medal if I could have. If I asked Juliet to get on a plane, she was off like a rocket. Christ, yes: off like a shot, fabulous. She adored adventure for its own sake. What she did was unquestionably always bloody good and very different.

She was enormously proud and didn't want the begging bowl: I liked and respected that. She was a nightmare to try to help. But, as she was always in financial difficulties, I advanced school fees and the like. Sometimes, up would come a request for more dosh – and on a fucking horse it went. She adored giving people presents – she loved the largesse. It was a pleasure to do it, and you knew that she would only ask if she was in trouble. She was not of this world, but there was a real heart there.

One of the many elements of why she was such a special person was her openness, her clarity. After we had known each other for a year or so, I asked her how Rory and she had met. She explained that she had just come back from Pakistan where her first husband had been killed and thought that she had reached the bottom. She said, 'I went to a wedding and met Rory, our eyes met, we went to bed, and stayed in bed for four days.' It sounds salacious, but it wasn't. I thought, 'Good on you.' That's all she said – you don't need any more. The honesty and straightforwardness was what I loved.

Right at the end, I gave her lunch at Ziani's [in London]. She was ill – very, very ill. I think she would have wanted to go out with a blaze of glory, not this dying of cancer. But I could see her being much more reflective and resigned to dying – calmer (you could spell that with a 'k' or a 'cal'), if you will. But I remember we did have half a guffaw. We knew that was the last we would see of each other, and she was dead six weeks later.

Re-creating the Great Game
Mike Reynolds

Born in Devon and educated at the Sorbonne and King's College Cambridge, Mike spent thirty years in the Foreign Service and was a co-founder of Hakluyt & Company in 1995. His latest book, Creating Der Rosenkavalier, *follows a BA and PhD in Opera Studies, his lifelong passion.*

The Cold War, which was the dominant political and strategic feature of most of my adult life, came to an extraordinarily undramatic end in the late 1980s. Understanding, countering and containing the Soviet Union and its allies wherever they were to be found in the world had been such an all-consuming task for the intelligence and security services of the Western world that prospects of a post-Cold War era seemed a bit unreal. What – exactly – were we all going to do when the major threat to Western democracy had simply petered out? And what was going to happen to the societies and the economies of all those client states once 'Moscow rules' no longer applied to them?

It took a little while, but a small group of like-minded colleagues from the secret world began to envisage a commercial opportunity in the new trade and investment patterns that slowly emerged in the 1990s. There were deals to be done and investments to be made in abundance in all those newly independent countries, eager to assert their freedom from their former Soviet masters. But the huge deficit was personal information and trust: who exactly were these potential new captains of Kazakh or Byelorussian or Uzbek industry and how could they be assessed? The answer – or part of it – lay in history, and the example of the nineteenth-century Great Game. For this had precise application to these very developments in the late twentieth century. What had to be done clearly needed to be organised privately, strictly commercially, well away from government and foreign policy considerations. What it would depend on more than anything was a network of independent, intrepid travellers who would go forth in search of relevant information. Retiring early from government service, two of us set about the private and commercial organisation of our new business venture and joined forces with three others. It was the late 1990s when we first began to think seriously about deploying our intrepid travellers to the countries where our first assignments took us; and into all five of our lives came Juliet.

Some of these countries surprised us. Juliet had expressed her willingness to return to Russia on our behalf as soon as we needed her there, but India and Pakistan interested her more, and she offered to work in Africa for us. Going through her extensive list of friends and contacts, acquired in unexpected and exotic ways during her momentous life to date, we found that she had interesting connections and prior knowledge in some surprising places. The fabled six degrees of separation are often an overstatement of the case. And so it was to Mumbai and to Delhi that we first sent her, not to Moscow or Dzerzhinsk. We relied on her ability to network and to think fast on her feet, to take sensible risks and to seize opportunities, to be that traveller of the Great Game era with a lively interest in the people and places she encountered, and to be a discreet collector of information and a purposeful follower of interesting leads. Juliet found she had a natural flair for the work, a 'nose' for the story behind the story, and took to our twentieth-century reinvention of Great Game techniques like a duck to water. In brief, she prospered.

Sometimes she met and worked with others in our rapidly developing network; mostly she worked alone. It was the latter she preferred. On an African assignment when she was working with a local 'expert', the authorities briefly detained both of them on spurious charges and asked for money. Juliet quickly cut a deal. But the local 'expert' stepped in and explained how things had to be done in that part of the world – an hour later, with the release fee now quadruple Juliet's original offer, she simply took the senior police officer aside, pressed her original cash offer into his hand, gave him a big smile and was allowed on her way. If theory and practice are separate skills, Juliet had the latter in abundance. She liked to do things and get on.

The techniques that our company developed were deceptively simple. Assignments were broken down into a

Juliet in Africa

series of specific questions – sometimes overlapping, sometimes not – and those questions were put to our travellers. I briefed Juliet for almost all of her assignments and found her refreshingly positive and practical. She saw instantly that by being in far-flung places, by seeking out and making friends, displaying empathy for their situation in the process, there was very little that she could not learn: her task was to ask, to listen and to remember. It helped that she liked many of the people whom she encountered, and they liked her; moreover, her instinctive feel for the Indian sub-continent gave her a head start in many of her assignments. Russia she found more problematic: she had lived previously in Moscow at a time of high drama, and personal tragedy, and her returns to that capital some time later were not her happiest experiences. But, practical as ever, Juliet always tried her hardest to find apposite answers to the questions we put to her. Her natural charm, and sense of humour, frequently came to her aid.

One of our earliest company mentors was Sir Fitzroy Maclean. It was he who stressed to us that the sort of information gathering we planned to do, using natural cover travellers with a sense of adventure all of their own, was nothing new. It just required a certain type of character: hardy, resilient, self-sufficient, but above all attractive to others. Juliet was precisely that type of character. Once instructed, briefed, equipped for her expedition, she was the ultimate self-starter: no need for encouraging words or exhortations along the way, you heard from Juliet once again when she had returned from the other side of the world and done the job.

Looking back, we were prompted by geo-political developments to take a risk, build a business and re-create the Great Game, for which we needed a network of remarkable people. How lucky we were, early on, to find Juliet and to be able to make use of her natural sense of adventure, her interest in people and her love of travel. In a nutshell, she was a delightful, inventive, humorous and courageous comrade-in-arms and business companion for well over a decade. Her contribution was immense.

In the Moscow Woods
Craig Kennedy

Craig Kennedy is co-chairman of the Pushkin House Trust.
A historian and former banker, he is currently writing a history
of Russian oil and how it shaped the arc of the Cold War.

It was an apt place to meet Juliet – a winter's evening in
Moscow in the waning years of the tumultuous 1990s. Friends
were throwing a dinner party at their rambling old dacha deep
in the wooded enclave of Serebrianyi Bor, a short drive from
the city centre. In times past, this district – an immense island
moated by the meandering arms of the Moscow river – had been
a preserve for falconry and horse breeding and later became a
weekend refuge for beleaguered Muscovites. Fading paint on
aged timbers, restrained *rezba* adorning eves and windows – an
oasis untouched by the storm reshaping the Russian landscape.
Were you looking to film Chekhov on location, this was the
place you would choose. It even had a cherry orchard that, like
the dacha itself, was not long for this world.

We ate in the conservatory, candlelight playing off the
frost-covered panes. Conversation invariably turned to Russia,
as we pondered its painful transformation. Sitting there, one
sensed this house was no stranger to such evenings, that it
had hosted generations of guests around its table, debating
Russia's destiny. Dacha talk was always freer talk; secreted in
the forest, one might dare to speak a truth.

Juliet, then a complete stranger to me, seemed at one with the place. In the company of strong personalities, she more than held her own. She was appalled by the political morass that Russia was sinking into. She was wryly sceptical of oligarchs and politicians. But she did not resort to easy orthodoxies and dismiss it all as hopeless. She asked probing questions, embraced complexity, and laughed at pomposity. Then, as later, I admired her ability to voice opinions robustly, but never stridently, and to temper them with an enquiring mind and a sense of humour.

We spoke together on and off throughout the evening. Juliet was then living in the UK and, at first, guarded about her reasons for visiting Moscow. As the evening wore on, she opened up a bit when she learned I had a passing knowledge of certain Russian business circles, sharing that she was there to investigate a joint venture gone sour. She asked if we could meet the next morning to discuss the matter and then set off to run the gauntlet of predatory traffic cops on the road to Peredelkino.

I was then working in Moscow in the hushed offices of a conservative American investment bank. Tangled up in our pinstripes, we were struggling to find our moorings in treacherous Russian waters. On my way to the meeting room next morning, I passed our unflappable receptionist who gave me an uncharacteristic look of wide-eyed astonishment. When I entered the room, I discovered why: there stood Juliet, resplendent in hunting breeches, boots, a black leather jacket and brandishing – if memory doesn't betray – a riding crop. Such a dashing figure had never before crossed our threshold. An Arabian among carthorses.

She outlined the all-too-familiar story: seasoned foreigners invest alongside supposedly solid Russian partners, who, in league with some dodgy Western associates, abscond with the money. In this case, there were some particularly tough characters involved. I was impressed by her pluck and knew her panache could provide a first line of defence in rough-and-tumble Moscow. But I wondered whether she had any idea what she might be getting herself into.

Only much later, when I had gotten to know Juliet, did I realise that she understood far better than a banker what risk taking really was – how bad things could turn out when you braved the odds and they turned against you. And I was moved by her courage and resilience: how she had overcome tragedy to return to the fray.

When Juliet left later that morning, I doubted I'd been much help. Indeed, she had certainly done more for me than I for her: office gossip about this formidable woman quickly spread, giving me some sorely needed cachet. As with anyone fortunate enough to know her, a bit of Juliet's elan always wore off on those around her.

We kept in touch. Eventually I moved to London, and when life in the city got too stifling, I would make the pilgrimage up to York Road Mews. Juliet's hospitality was always the perfect tonic – countryside, good company, a stack of fresh titles from her beloved Heywood Hill inviting us to revive our minds. At the end of the day, Juliet would herd us to her great round dinner table, where the salmon was poached and the guests well grilled. The dacha reborn in Yorkshire.

Some years later, back in Moscow, I went looking for that house in Serebranyi Bor. My friends had long since left the country, and Juliet was no longer with us. The dacha, along with its stand of cherries, had been buried by the developer's bulldozer to make way for the faux imperial mansions of the new elite.

The feeling of loss was acute. An age of enchantment had passed, yielding to a harsher time, one in need of Juliet's kind of fearless commitment to difficult causes. In this new world, it's sometimes tempting to give in to despair. And when that happens, it helps to recall Juliet's voice – with that admonishment all-too-familiar, I'm sure, to Fynn and Lettice – saying 'that's not on!' Which means it's time to buck up, wade back into the fray and find some worthy odds to brave.

Dented but Not Undermined
Tom Rhodes

Before working for Hakluyt, Tom was a journalist and had encountered Juliet's second husband, Rory, in Bosnia. He met her in 2001, six years before her death.

I will never forget our first meeting. I had just joined a strategic consultancy in Mayfair where Juliet consulted on an occasional basis. We worked in an elegant London townhouse, an unusually civilised oasis where we would meet those who helped us in the field to discuss our various projects around the world.

On this occasion, I wandered down the staircase from our offices with some trepidation. Juliet was known throughout the building as one of the best people at our disposal – and I had no idea what to expect, other than being told that she was bright, fearfully glamorous and wore an eye patch. My first glimpse of her in a long brown leather skirt, talking in an animated but quite imperious voice, did little to dispel my fears.

We were introduced and walked back upstairs to a first-floor sitting room to discuss our shared project. As I went through the detail and Juliet took notes, I started to relax and so did she. The encounter ended, as was so often the case with Juliet, in uproarious laughter – and from that moment on I would not only look forward to our many subsequent meetings, but knew that they would be the most uplifting moments of any day.

We would discuss the many countries that we had visited, the journalists we knew and had known, and the excitement of the hunt that imbued her very being – in every sense. She would regale me with tales from her travels. She would present me with gifts from far-flung lands. All of these came with a humorous twist: I still own the ivory chopsticks she had managed to smuggle out of Africa on my behalf.

Juliet, naturally, had no truck with political correctness in any form. But this did not mean she lacked sensitivity. Over numerous lunches she revealed much about her own life. The loss of two husbands had dented but not undermined her deep faith. At a very fundamental level she cared about people – and that was why she was so adept at finding often delicate information, whether about the inner workings of a Russian oligarch's family, the tribal leanings of a Nigerian potentate, or even the internecine conflicts of her neighbours in Tadcaster.

Above all, she was very brave. Even as her illness began to take an ever stronger hold, she would telephone from wherever she was at the time – walking up a German mountain while on some special alternative diet, for example, or from her London base in Connaught Square – to argue about the current state of British or Russian political life, or the threat to her beloved hunting from the 'antis'. In typically selfless fashion, she was the first to send me a letter of condolence when my father died. I had moved on by then to another company where Juliet once again became a mainstay in researching some of our more difficult endeavours in interesting parts of the world.

We would meet for what she described as 'illegal' bacon rolls at a small café on Connaught Street: the free spirit in her would not allow Juliet to stick to her medically advised diet at all costs. 'There's really nothing better than a bacon roll,' she would say, before launching into a scything analysis of the Tory Party. I imagine her now, sitting on her heavenly cloud, having much the same thought today.

Border Incident
Mouse Campbell

Mouse met Juliet through his wife, Georgiana. They travelled with Juliet and her son Fynn to Afghanistan, and he with Juliet to Kazakhstan and Uzbekistan, towards the end of her life.

I felt so sorry for the man from the embassy. He was trying to persuade Juliet to return to England and abandon a trip to the Wakhan Corridor, a thin strip of land high in the Pamirs, where China, Pakistan and Tajikistan meet Afghanistan. It was a summer's evening in 2004. Afghanistan was more or less peaceful, but quite often less rather than more. She appeared to be listening attentively and if one didn't know her, amenably. It was pretty dark in the garden of the Gandamack Lodge in Kabul, but not dark enough to miss the flash of mischief in Juliet's eye as the intelligence officer made his case.

Even he seemed to admit defeat since he concluded his pleadings by warning that if she did go, she should travel in a blacked-out vehicle, under no circumstances should take any interest in any of the poppy fields that we would travel through, and should stay safely in towns after nightfall. Within twenty-four hours Juliet had gleefully broken all three rules: the last by insisting on sleeping in the car on a small and diminishing island in a flooding river miles from any habitation. Our dinner celebrating this final infraction was a fruitcake I had bought at the Cranborne village fête.

Very early on in my friendship with Juliet I noticed her bark. It was a single, sharp 'Ha!' that was invariably deployed with devastating effect. You always knew exactly what it meant, although at any particular time it could mean anything: that's rubbish; that's cheap; that's humbug; that's pathetic; that's ugly; that's underhand; that's 'United Nations' etcetera etcetera. The first time I noticed it, it was being used at me over dinner in my own house to pass judgement on my (lack of) knowledge of Afghanistan. It was over this dinner that the first plans to venture to the Wakhan were laid.

The plans were preposterous and terrifying from the start. Juliet, however, had absolute faith that everything would be fine. When the Taleban attacked and killed an unfortunate party of Chinese engineers who were building the road that we were to travel along a week later, Juliet deemed this a jolly good thing since she thought it meant it less likely that there would be another attack in the same area for a while. Her approach to logistics was simply to circumvent any problem: at the time the only way to get from Islamabad to Kabul by air was by a UN flight that was available only to aid-workers, not civilians. Juliet solved this by appointing us to unusual roles in a friendly Afghan charity. And so it was that our particular flight had on its roster a Mouse Trainer and a Mouse Herder.

It was three hot days' drive from Kabul to Sarhadt, where we were to pick up our horses and mules. Whilst out hunting in Dorset, Juliet had met a consultant to the Home Office who was senior adviser to Tony Blair's drug eradication programme. So senior was he that he was not allowed to leave Kabul on his trips to Afghanistan although, to Juliet's considerable delight, he had gone on field trips to remote parts of Hampshire to see opium poppies being grown for the NHS. He said that the Home Office did not have reliable data on the price of poppy as it made its journey from the fields, through the refineries as heroin, to export. Within three days of leaving Kabul, Juliet had assembled and cross-checked prices of seed, fertiliser and product in all the provinces we travelled through, as well as practical tips for an efficient harvest. The man from the embassy would have been aghast if he had seen her threading her way through the mauve, white and blue poppies in her Emma Hope shoes, taking lessons from the farmers on the correct angle to hold a poppy comb. I don't think she had any other purpose in this other than to have something to tease the Home Office about the next time she went out with the Wilton Hunt.

Juliet appointed herself quartermaster of the expedition. In Faizabad, the last town of any size that we were to pass through, she set off into the bazaar with our guide, Haji (whom she had already marked as a colossal bore) to get provisions. A long time later and after a lot of haggling, she emerged with our entire stores for our weeks in the wilderness: a sack of rice and a sack of somewhat melancholy onions.

Kunduz 2004. Mouse Campbell with Haji, the interpreter, three Afghans, Fynn, Georgiana Campbell, and a young Afghan

There is a wonderful freedom in the remoteness of the Wakhan and its vast, brutal landscape. It is no accident that almost any Westerner who goes there feels compelled to write about it and invariably claims to be the first white man to set foot there since the days of the Great Game. I think we tacitly also succumbed to this feeling. I only ever saw Juliet look vaguely discombobulated once, when, after days of riding without seeing anyone but our small band of horsemen, we rounded a corner to find a party of Japanese tourists coming in the other direction. We all pretended not to have seen each other.

It was an extremely uncomfortable trip. In the high thirties during the cloudless days, the temperature would fall away very quickly after sunset to well below freezing. Some of the passes we travelled over were above sixteen thousand feet, our horses disappearing into snow up to their withers. Juliet always turned out of her tent in the morning looking like she was going out to lunch somewhere smart in Gloucestershire. This made a marked impression on our horsemen, all of whom were in awe of her, although her refusal to compromise elegance with prudence meant that she did on occasion succumb to sunstroke.

Towards the end of our ride, we were detained by the Pakistani army for attempting to cross the border in a restricted military zone. The senior officer, a softly spoken rather short man with bottle-lensed spectacles, ordered us to return to Kabul. We had neither the money nor the inclination. For a moment it looked like he would lock us up, but the only cell in the fort was extensively populated by a large colony of rather amiable bees. Instead he had his men point their elderly .303s at us and ordered us to move. Juliet sat down. He ordered us to strike the one tent we had put up. Juliet, from a sitting position, started to peg out a second one. Infuriated, the officer and one of his men grabbed the youngest member of our party, Fynn, who was then fifteen, by the arms. With a considerable amount of effort they pulled him to his feet. He towered over them both. Juliet sprang to her feet and advanced on the wretched officer. 'Get your hands off my son. The Pakistani army is attacking an unarmed boy. I wish to make a complaint. I demand that you summon the British Ambassador here this instant!' The officer and his men scuttled back into their fort to report their defeat to higher authority.

'Ha!' barked Juliet.

Christmas in Timbuktu
Tim Pope

Tim, a lawyer, met Juliet through Charlotte Black at an exhibition at Harewood House in 1994. She asked him for advice concerning a sponsorship contract with Sony for the Rory Peck Trust, and they became friends.

In the summer of 2002, Juliet announced she was planning a Christmas trip to Timbuktu – in the same way most of us would say we were going to Devon. She never revealed why she wanted to go, save that it was a desire going back to her childhood.

Slightly reluctantly, I found myself landing at Bamako airport with Juliet, Fynn, Lettice and Craig, Fynn's half-brother from California. In those days, Bamako airport was a very large, corrugated-iron shed. After much confusion we went off to spend the first night in what was, by Mali standards, a luxury hotel. This was far too touristy for Juliet and she quickly negotiated for a local boatman to take us up the Niger river to Timbuktu.

The boat was a basic affair, the lavatorial arrangements limited to a plank with a hole in it suspended off the back of the boat. Lunch and dinner was largely grilled fish and we camped onshore at night, Juliet and Lettice in a tent and the rest of us under the stars in sleeping bags. Juliet always insisted we had to moor far away from any other boats to avoid being regarded as common tourists.

It was a magical trip – sunny days, lounging on cushions watching the countryside slide by, reading and chatting about matters grave and not, stopping at riverside villages to buy fish and French-style baguettes. Lettice was engrossed in one of her many Harry Potter books for most of the river trip and on being told we were passing a baby hippo, looked up from her book and grunted, 'Oh, a hippo!' and then buried her nose back in Harry.

We were booked in to the best hotel in Timbuktu. Its most notable features were dust, sand, broken air-conditioning units and a fax machine, and more dust. Juliet insisted we had our passports stamped on arrival as she had read that there was a night club in New York where admission was free if you had a 'Tomboctou' stamp in your passport, and she was keen to see if it was true.

Juliet wanted to venture as quickly as possible into the desert on camels. Waiting in reception on a (broken) sofa

Lettice, Fynn, Juliet and Tim Pope on camels near Timbuktu

was a striking-looking Tuareg tribesman in traditional blue robes. He was not at all keen on negotiating the details with Juliet as she was a woman, but after I had failed to reduce the ridiculously high price, she stepped in. After half an hour of hard negotiating she had reduced the price to a fraction of his opening gambit.

We set off the next day with a very grumpy guide: not only had Juliet reduced his price to what he regarded as an insult, she had also informed him she did not eat meat, so the daily rice dish was to be vegetarian. As the elder man of the party I was given the best and fastest camel – this upset Lettice, who felt she should have been on him, as clearly she was the best rider. Although we did not get very far into the desert in the three-day trip, it was amazingly beautiful, very peaceful and very still. Juliet loved it – we did not see any tourists or indeed any other people at all, just some smugglers' jeeps crossing the desert at night.

Timbuktu 2002. Craig Vergos, Lettice, Tim Pope and Fynn

Nightly suppers were rice and vegetables, mixed up in a filthy enamel bowl by our guide, cooked on the fire; water was very limited so was not wasted on washing hands or cooking utensils which were cleaned with sand. Fynn, Craig and I all slept on surprisingly comfortable sand under the stars. Juliet and Lettice slept in a tent, from which Juliet emerged every morning looking amazingly stylish. She had the ability to make whatever she wore look very chic whether she was in Notting Hill or the middle of the Sahara.

We arrived back in Timbuktu on Christmas Day. We were looking forward, with some slight trepidation, to the hotel's special Christmas dinner that evening. Sadly they had served it on Christmas Eve so we had a slightly more sophisticated version of the Tuareg suppers with half a cardboard box of very old musty red wine which they had found in a cupboard.

We stayed for the final night in Mali. Lettice ended up having dinner on the other side of the dining room with some missionaries' children and their parents. She did not appear to stop talking to them or at them for the entire dinner. Afterwards the mother remarked to Juliet what a vivid imagination Lettice had as she had informed them over dinner that Juliet had no husband at the moment as both of them had been shot. Juliet laughed it off with genuine mirth and said Lettice had probably been reading too much Harry Potter.

Laughter is my abiding memory of Juliet. She was only sad when she spoke of Rory – she once told me that she carried a packet of his letters with her wherever she went in the world, and thought about him every day.

MAINE

A Sort of Sanctuary
Tanya Swaine

*Tanya's husband, Sherwood Swaine, had been good friends
with Rory Peck for many years. Sherwood and Tania lived
on Clearwater Lake where Rory bought a house, Lyon's Lair,
with his first wife Janey. After Rory's death, Juliet brought
large groups of friends every summer to the house, a tradition
Fynn and Lettice have continued.*

Thinking about Juliet makes me smile. She was courageous
and determined, generous and funny, and sometimes, in
Maine, very vulnerable and alone. Sherwood used to fly a
floatplane and we all decided to fly up to a remote lake for a
weekend camping adventure.

Lyon's Lair, now called Camp Liberty, in Maine

Rory and Juliet's camp, Lyon's Lair, was a turn-of-the-century former hunting lodge down the shore from Sherwood's home. They were staying at the camp with Rory's two sons, Jamie and Ali, Fynn, and baby Lettice, and had secured a sitter for the weekend. Juliet was exceptionally calm and collected, and Rory and she would banter, exchanging mild insults couched in the most endearing language – usually introduced with 'Darling ...'

We had fantastic weather – all blue skies and beautiful temperatures. We flew to an island on the lake, set up camp there and Sherwood secured us a small boat. The airplane was tied up to trees and on our first night we woke in the middle of the night to the sounds of something very large near the tents. A moose had decided to come ashore where the plane was secured, and had got tangled in the ropes. There was a bit of a panic that the moose would either damage the plane or trample us in our tents. There was little we could do, but

Rory and Juliet on the balcony in Maine in the early 1990s

fortunately the moose sorted himself out and went on his way. I'm not sure that Juliet was a great fan of the actual camping but we were all very young and in love at the time. Before we left the island, we put a bottle of wine in a hole in a tree. That summer was the last we would see Rory.

It was a couple of years after Rory died that Juliet got in touch to say that she was coming to Maine. On that trip, she came alone and tried to sort out legal matters around the camp. She had already been through so much in her life and she was unbelievably stoic about it all. She seemed to love Maine and I think had a vision of the camp serving as a sort of sanctuary. She came nearly every year after that and eventually would bring Fynn and Lettice and then many of their friends as well. They seemed to love it, having dinners at the camp with a gaggle of young people always up to some adventure, like fishing for a bass using a spear, building traps for eels or hunting rodents.

Maine 1992–3. Rory, Fynn, Ali and Jamie on a bullfrog hunt

Then Juliet started to rent out the camp, and her time here involved a flurry of sorting and improvements to the house, as it was uninsulated and had been largely unoccupied for years. There were mice and squirrels in the attic, and the occasional wood rat. For a time, Sherwood and I helped manage the bookings and renters. Characteristically, Juliet was dismissive of the frivolous whims – some not so petty – of the renters:

when one family complained about bats, Juliet suggested that we should charge extra for wildlife – it was part of the experience.

Years after that first camping trip in Parmachenee, Sherwood recovered the bottle of wine we left in the tree and gave it to Juliet. When she was in Maine, we always enjoyed at least one evening with her over a bottle of wine or a couple of scotches. Her amazing experiences lent perspective to our own. A couple of summers before she passed, she brought over an old pressback rocking chair; she had had the seat redone and gave it to Sherwood. It's on our front porch looking over the lake.

Not Your Average Nanny's Job
Kirsten Chambers-Taylor

Kirsten lived in New Zealand before obtaining a visa to Britain, where she worked for Juliet for a year and a half. She currently works at the British Consulate in Boston.

I first met Juliet in a pub in Battersea in the spring of 1995, when I was twenty-five. She was interviewing me for a job as a live-in nanny and horse-wrangler. I'm sure I dressed appropriately, but Juliet was in leather pants, cowboy boots and a Versace eye patch. 'Do you like kids?' she asked. 'Yeah, sure.' 'Great,' she said. And that was it.

Sometimes it takes a new nanny a few weeks to discover her place within the family's pecking order. But on my first day, as we enjoyed a cup of tea and a slice of cake at the kitchen table, Lettice (three and a half years old at the time) decided to show me that she had absolute power over her Mummy. Giving me a sly look and sliding her hand into the butter dish, she squelched the soft butter between her fingers. Before I could think, I reached out and slapped her hand, then carried on drinking my tea. Lettice was horrified and looked to her mother for help. But Juliet just smiled and said, 'Well, I wouldn't do that again, Lettice.'

Ten days after I arrived, Juliet took a trip to the US, leaving me alone with Fynn and Lettice for two weeks. This didn't faze me and seemed quite natural to her. She travelled a good deal, and would regularly be gone for more than a week with no notice, having been 'deployed' with her investigative work. When home, she would bury herself in her attic office with Russian classical music blaring, sip Russian Caravan or Lapsang Souchong tea (Fortnum & Mason, of course) and work feverishly on building the Rory Peck Trust.

She had an Arab stallion that she brought with her from Russia. Brownie was a feisty chestnut who grew about five feet when riled. That was often. He would frighten the neighbour's horses by screaming at the mares from across the fence, and once, after dumping Juliet down the road, mounted the gate. Sometimes I had to go out and look for Juliet, and when I'd find her – ego bruised, but otherwise fine – she would greet me with a rueful smile. 'It was my fault,' she would laugh. And the next day, off she would go again, right as rain. Bowing to

Maine, probably 1995. Jamie Peck, Fynn, Lettice, Craig Vergos, Ali Peck, Nathalie Vergos. This was the only time that all Rory and Dominique's children were together

neighbourhood pressure, she had Brownie gelded. We did it in the field, me helping the vet by holding him while he was sedated. Juliet couldn't watch. It gutted her to have to do this – she was a fan of true spirit, whether it be human or animal. She knew character when she saw it.

Juliet cared deeply for all her animals. At the Mews one afternoon I heard Fynn shouting for help. Running outside we saw Juliet's Boston terrier Harry tied to the apple tree. When Fynn climbed the tree, he had disturbed the nest and the poor dog was swarmed with wasps. Without hesitating, Juliet covered her head in a coat and waded into the swarm to rescue Harry. He must have been stung fifty times. After this, he clung to Juliet like a small child, so desperate to be close to her that he would snarl at me when I tried to separate them to give her a break. I remember calling him 'needy', but Fynn rejected that, saying it was 'loyalty'.

I travelled light in those days – a backpack and sports bag held all my belongings. Juliet told me that ignorance can present itself in fancy clothes just as surely as wisdom can be found walking around in ragged pants. That lesson stuck.

In December 1995, we – Juliet and I and the six children, Fynn, Lettice, Alexander and Jamie Peck, Craig and Nathalie Vergos – went to Camp Liberty in Farmington, Maine. We arrived in the middle of the night after a long, snow-hobbled journey to find the property buried under snowdrifts. The driveway was impassable, so we packed all our luggage and supplies on to the kids' plastic toboggans and towed them the mile or so downhill to the gingerbread cabin in the woods. Camp Liberty was very important to Juliet – she felt close to Rory there and was able to still her mind. The kids loved the freedom and would fish, shoot, ski, ice skate, toboggan and play the fool. I can still imagine Juliet sitting in the rocking chair on the landing outside her room, reading and shaking her head at the kids' antics. That trip the pipes froze, so all water had to be brought up from the lake and boiled. Juliet, Nathalie and I took turns bringing buckets of water up to make tea, wash dishes and boil the lobsters – Juliet wouldn't let a visit pass without Maine lobster. Friends came from Boston and all around the area to stay – the trip was ten days of at times about ten adults and ten kids, wet boots, cooking, dishes, and clearing up. After dinner, we listened to everyone talking about politics, the economy, religion and international affairs in front of the massive stone fireplace.

When the time came to produce the first Rory Peck Awards, budgets were tight. The brochure was to be produced in German, French and English, yet they couldn't afford translators or typesetters: step-daughter Nathalie translated into French, another friend into German, and I typed the descriptions of entrants and winners in three languages. Juliet knew how to seize the moment, sometimes to the anxiety of her partners. Hearing that there was a meeting in Montreal to talk about insurance for freelance journalists, she scrambled with colleagues in London to whip up a video to showcase the needs of freelancers. We couriered it to Montreal and I arranged for the other village nanny's mother, who lived there, to hand-deliver the package to the conference for us.

I lived in Healaugh for only eighteen months, but she shaped the person I am today. Juliet taught me diplomacy, resilience and compassion. Her compassion was bottomless, from exiled religious clerics, to stranded Afghan boxers whose train tickets to come to Healaugh she would pay for, to those who pursued her affections, to her beloved kids and dogs. She was always calm, always respectful and always wry, despite so much going on personally behind the scenes.

A Holiday in Maine
James Clarke

*James is a school friend of Juliet's son Fynn, with whom he
shared a boarding house at Marlborough College. He is now
a lawyer working in the City.*

I spent a fortnight with Fynn at their camp in Maine. The
house and its proximity to the water, hammocks fastened
to the trees and a fridge full of Samuel Adams beer boded
a well-deserved and relaxing holiday spent recovering from
exam stress. This was not to be. Juliet, aided by her gifted but

*Maine 2000–1. Jessie Crawley, Freddie Watson, Zac Crawley, George Head, Fynn,
Grandpa, Minnie Crawley, Mo Crawley, Lettice. Summer holidays were spent
messing around in boats on the lake*

draconian lieutenant Fynn, had us earning our keep throughout with a medley of odd-jobs: assembling beds, cheffing and harpooning bass from the lake for supper. But she believed in rewarding hard work: downtime on the speedboat, memorable suppers of lobster and brazen and frequent purchases of alcohol for minors.

She didn't exactly play by the rules. My query as to whether I was insured on the left-hand-drive truck (at least five times larger than any other car I'd driven) was firm and non-committal in equal measure – I didn't need to worry. I'd not even negotiated the long driveway before darting left (rather than right), and very narrowly missed colliding head-on with a truck. Upon witnessing this near-miss, there was no sharp intake of breath, no squeal of panic. She just laughed loudly and went back to her shopping list. This was a trait Juliet probably most frequently demonstrated during her life – a commendable devil-may-care attitude and a fierce hardiness.

A Nephew's Perspective
Thomas Bromet

Thomas is a conservation architect for Donald Insall Associates, and has worked on buildings such as the Bank of England, Kew Gardens and Westminster Palace. He is a very good friend of Fynn's, and his cousin by marriage.

Aged seven or so, Fynn and I were always making army bases in the header rows and fields near the Mews. To

Maine 2002–3. Rebuilding the boathouse. Fynn, Silas Crawley, Joseph Ridley, Thomas Bromet

help form one of these bases, Fynn was drilling into a piece of wood outside. He accidentally drilled into his thumb – it made a perfect hole, so that you could see through it. He went in to see Juliet, who was entertaining a guest in her drawing room. He pointed out the hole in his thumb. She said that he would be fine, and should carry on.

When Juliet got Fynn a new passport, it had the wrong date of birth on it. Fynn accidentally took this with him to Maine, and she had to blag him through border control. She may have forgotten Fynn's date of birth, but by sheer force of personality, she got him through.

Once, we turned up – really late – to the airport in Boston to fly home from Maine. There were about twenty of us, all in different rental cars, and it was chaos. Juliet jumped every queue there was, checked in, and went straight to the front of the security queue. She just had an air and a way that made anything seem possible. I was too young to really appreciate how she did it. I wish I had paid more attention.

CANCER AND LAST YEARS

An Outrageous Patron
Nick Clarke

Ill for ten years after a breakdown at university, Nick, a self-taught craftsman, set up on his own in York in the 1990s. He met Juliet through one of her Wighill neighbours, Isabel Denyer, who held an open house for local craftsmen.

It was almost the first opportunity like that for me, a struggling, budding young craftsman. Juliet happened to come and it wasn't long before I got a phone call from her. I ended up going to see her at York Road Mews. She was the most outrageous person I've ever met. Although I had gone to university, I was quite a simple guy and I'd never met anyone like Juliet. She recognised things in people that others don't see; she looked way beyond what she perceived she might like, and saw the story behind it. Why did that guy stick marbles in his furniture, why did he use stained glass, why were all the bits of wood contrasting in colours and why was there so much texture?

I was forever at the house – the phone would go and she would say that she needed something, ridiculous things from bookcases to a kitchen plate rack, coat hooks made from old taps, old forks and spoons. She loved anything I did and largely left the ideas up to me. Side tables, mirror frames, wardrobes that had Eastern flavours with marbles highlighting things and glass. We worked together, but she'd also let me go. It was a great opportunity for someone who had never been able to express himself. She was a patron.

For me, just being at the house was something else. The first day I went there, Fynn and Letty were very young. I was trying to make head or tail of this bizarre woman, her crazy house and two screaming kids and dogs everywhere. Fynn came up to me and said, 'My dad's dead. He was shot, you know.' Two minutes later, Letty ran up to me and said, 'My dad's dead too. And he was shot too.' Obviously they were not happy about it, but it was matter-of-fact.

Her whole house was fascinating. The first thing that hit you was the smell of wet dog and the things that they ate; then there was the mothbally smell in the furniture. Then there was just the intensity of living, or a life that had been lived. The office – piles of papers and pictures and films and photographs and cameras, and a desk that you knew would never see the light of day, files bursting and stuff pouring out.

Fynn, Juliet and Lettice, Healaugh 2005–6. Our last Christmas photograph

And then there was the red room with the huge head of Lenin and the most dramatic, heroic paintings on the walls. The whole place reeked of people whose stories were fabulous, who had seen and witnessed things that mere mortals couldn't even talk about or imagine. Rugs and cushions, pictures and photographs of people on horseback, people with cameras slung over their shoulder. And she was there – she was one of those people in those pictures.

We didn't have long chats. I'm an out and out born-again Christian and I take every opportunity to talk about the Lord. Our friendship reminded me of the story in the bible about King Saul, Jonathan and David, where Jonathan uses a boy to signal to David that his life was in danger. David's life was saved, and the witless boy was used to achieve that aim. I felt like that boy. An incidental person who unknowingly was fundamental in some huge decisions in somebody's life.

She would be seriously ill and you wouldn't know it. I remember right towards the end I gave her a big hug, and afterwards I realised that she was in excruciating pain because of what I had done. She never let on.

And of course, there were all those attempts to find out what she did. I tried every time. 'So what is it that you do?' She'd tell me, but I never knew exactly what it was. It did occur to me that she did something that was a bit peculiar – it sounded like industrial espionage.

At the funeral, I asked Priscilla, 'Was she a spy?' She said: 'Oh yes, of course she was. If you look round the room, there are dozens of them here.' I looked round and the people in the room were like people from a Bond movie. Glamorous as anything, but stories etched in their faces and clothes to match.

A Doctor's View

Mark Denyer

Mark and Juliet's families had known each other for many years, having first met through evangelical Christian circles during the war. The Denyers moved to Yorkshire in 1982.

Juliet moved to Healaugh in the mid-1990s following Rory's tragic death in Moscow. I think Letty was about a year old and Fynn a few years older. My first contact with Juliet, as far as I can remember, was through her retro-orbital cancer, which had been diagnosed the previous year and as a result of which she had lost her eye. I am a gastroenterologist, so know very little about such tumours. At Juliet's request I discussed her case with relevant colleagues. They told me that this type of tumour was particularly nasty, and that she needed radiotherapy. Fortunately, I was able to put her in touch with a friend and colleague who is a superb oncologist and he did a wonderful job in curing her cancer completely. She then needed hyperbaric oxygen therapy to her eye socket in order to strengthen the bone for a potential glass eye in future but of course, being Juliet, she decided not to bother with this and thereafter ensured that she took maximum advantage of her black patch. So, 'She's got her eye on you,' as an election slogan when standing for local councillor.

We became very good friends with Juliet. She was highly intelligent and also wise, qualities which too rarely go together. She was a woman of strong opinions but they were always well thought through. One example concerned 'home schooling'. Juliet thought her sister Priscilla was completely mad to insist on this for her four girls and I gather she made her opinion on the matter crystal clear. We happened to agree with Juliet – but of course could say nothing to Priscilla! Fynn and Letty went to Red House, a very small school a few villages away run by a most singular couple. They were very happy there and clearly received a good educational grounding. Juliet used to drive them at high speed in whatever car she had at the time, tearing along narrow country roads in what many considered a most dangerous fashion. But she was a very good driver and, as far as I know, never had an accident whilst living here.

Juliet was a very beautiful woman. She had wonderful cheekbones, a lovely remaining eye, a slim figure and good legs. She dressed well, often a little unconventionally but always tastefully. I was thoroughly smitten, as I know were many men. She enjoyed beautiful things and was always appreciative of small gifts such as a nice bunch of flowers. She enjoyed a drink, but never to excess, and always had a stock of the delicious Jupiter's Field sparkling wine, made by a cousin who had a vineyard in Sussex. I remember once sitting outside her house on a summer evening, just chatting, watching the swallows and enjoying a glass or two – a small but precious moment.

It was an enormous sadness that my last links with Juliet once again involved cancer. She telephoned me in, I think, the autumn of 2001 and told me without preamble, 'Mark, I've got bowel cancer.' Tragically, this had been missed a good six months earlier, so I was very concerned. I arranged for her care to be transferred to Leeds, which is the local teaching hospital centre, and a colleague operated to remove the tumour. Whilst this was technically successful, unfortunately the growth had invaded some local blood vessels and this was to prove ultimately fatal. Juliet started post-operative chemotherapy, which statistically would have significantly improved her chances of a complete cure; however for some reason, and against the advice of friends and family, she abandoned this and decided to go for alternative therapy. She didn't ask for my opinion about this and, knowing that she would have made up her mind very firmly, I did not offer it, which was perhaps cowardly of me. But I don't think I'd have managed to dissuade her from her chosen course.

All went well for about four years, but in the summer of 2006 she came for dinner on my birthday and clearly had a nasty cough. I feared the worst and advised her to go for a chest x-ray, which confirmed lung secondaries. The writing was now on the wall, as all that could now be offered was palliative therapy. Later she developed bone metastases, some of which were horrid to look at. She remained incredibly cheerful and positive but went downhill rapidly and after that I saw very little of her, though we received regular updates from Priscilla. Our last meeting was in church on Christmas Day 2006. I hardly recognised her, so disfigured had she become as a result of her steroid treatment. Gone were those wonderful high cheekbones, the slender form and the beautiful legs. But it was very much the old Juliet smiling out at us. She died just two weeks later. Priscilla phoned me at work to tell me. I could not help crying. A very special light had gone out.

But although Juliet's death only a few weeks before her forty-sixth birthday was, humanly speaking, a tragedy, from the heavenly perspective it was very far from that. During those final few agonising months she finally came through to a very real personal faith in Jesus, something which I think she had resisted for many years but which she at the end embraced wholeheartedly. She was in a way that sheep which was lost but whom her Lord found and gently restored. She died at peace, and at one with Him, and for that reason my memories of her, although coloured with enormous sadness at losing her so young, are at the same time full of joy, and of profound gratitude at having had the great privilege of knowing her.

Forward Planning
Milly Soames

Milly and Juliet's paths had only crossed occasionally since their years in the sixth form of Marlborough College.

Juliet sat at our kitchen table sporting an eye patch, sounding like Marie Colvin and looking like Lady Gaga. Twenty years or so had passed and then out of the blue she asked herself to supper (the highest form of flattery), and I sat

Juliet and Lettice, Healaugh 2005

captivated by her stories of life in Moscow and Kabul. She talked very openly of Fynn and Lettice and her husbands, but less openly of her work. I had known from mutual friends of her illness so I was prepared for the eye patch, but we were not close and Facebook for the middle-aged had not really kicked in and I doubt whether Juliet would have used it.

Looking back on that evening I am sure Juliet engineered it because she knew she was not going to get over the cancer. I think she had done her homework and through friends and family knew my daughter Daisy was the same age as Lettice, and that they shared a love of horses and hunting. Juliet was, I believe, actively broadening the scope of people who would take an interest in Lettice and I am so very grateful that we made the cut and Lettice wanted to spend time with us once Juliet had died.

Lettice and Daisy became good friends. Lettice took Daisy with her to stay with her godmother, Catherine Cairns, on her farm in South Africa when they were only thirteen. They were to have three more wonderful trips to Uitgedacht before summers had to be spent on internships. Catherine was immensely kind and also quite strict with them, so they were up and out helping with the ponies and having a wonderful time learning how to play polo.

Lettice is as independent as her mother and happily we see her when her busy life allows.

Reconciliation
Silas Crawley

Silas is Juliet's younger brother. They overlapped for two years when at Marlborough College. After she left the UK for Peshawar and then Moscow they saw each other little more than annually.

We weren't close, but neither were we deliberately distant. I never fell out with Julie. But I did keep my distance, desperate to avoid conflict, and a little bit afraid of her sharp tongue. After Dominique's tragic death, Annie and I visited Julie in Peshawar and we had a wonderful time. She was always so generous, and always so interested in our lives.

***

I recall the dismissive way in which she spoke to a young Pakistani petrol pump attendant. 'Go away, little man,' she said to him as he stared at her and lingered by the car after filling the car up with petrol. You can't speak to people like that, I thought to myself. But then I didn't understand what it was like to be a Western woman in that culture, and she did.

***

During the late 1980s and early 1990s I was in a band that had a good deal of success, although we never 'hit the big time'. If Julie was in the country she would make an effort to come to our gigs, and she always purchased a plenteous supply of the band merchandise. Just like our grandfather and father, she was always generous. She would never just buy a T-shirt for herself, but would get loads more for her friends.

Julie loved and was hugely generous to our children. On one occasion, in order to support a fundraising event that her nephew Zac was involved in, she told me to top all other bids for his graffiti canvas, despite not having seen it at all. In the end I think she donated a hundred pounds for a small canvas – generous to the extreme.

***

When we lived in different countries, despite our physical separation, we were able to enjoy occasional times together because we both had a mutual admiration for what each other was doing. Once the seriousness of her cancer became clear, I received an email from Julie which summed up her feelings towards me. It read as follows:

> It has for a long time been a great sadness to me that I see so little of you and your wonderful family. It is the way that we live, both you and I. Our commitments to others and a way of life. But it is a sadness that I hold. I am a massive admirer of yours. I think that what you do and have done is most remarkable.

For me these words were both poignant and surprising, coming from a woman who was unbelievably courageous and inspiring herself. I deeply regret that it was only at the very end of her life, indeed the last fifteen months, that we were able to express our true feelings for one another. Both of us had an inbuilt compassion for those on the edges of society. I remember discussing with Julie how to best help those who found themselves in the prison of addiction or were homeless. We shared stories of people we were trying to help, laughed at our own naïveté and botched efforts, but resolved to keep trying. It was this common concern to help those in distress that fuelled our mutual admiration.

***

Julie and I shared a common faith in God. For most of our lives we expressed this in very different ways. I am naturally quite extrovert and have often been associated with the 'happy-clappy lot'; Julie was comfortable with a more private expression of her beliefs. It was hilarious when we attended church together in the last couple of years of her life: she would dress up for the occasion and I would be in jeans and a T-shirt and trainers; I would greet people in the 'Peace' part of the service and she would remain seated and announce to anyone wishing to shake her hand that, 'this is a peace-free zone'! But we both knew that true faith is not about how you behave in church for one hour a week, it's about how you express your love for God by who you are, and what you do in the other 167 hours of the week.

***

Julie's illness humbled us as a family. We could no longer avoid talking about things that had lain dormant and unresolved. I knew that I had much to answer for in my own relationship with Julie. I wrote this to her in an email on 6 December 2005, the day after she had received a particularly gloomy scan report:

> *I am fully aware that I have to my shame often been a very distant brother. In recent months I have become very aware of how self-sufficient and independent I have been for many years. I am so sorry that I have been so distant particularly because you have been so kind to all of us, especially with all the fabulous holidays* [Julie used to invite us annually to Maine, USA].

Julie's response was very kind, affirming and forgiving. For her, the holidays were a wonderful way in which she could practically reconnect with us as a family. Our gratitude to our parents, who enabled the holidays to happen, was huge.

As the cancer took a greater grip on Julie's body so our times of deepening friendship increased. The walls between us all, as siblings within one family, came tumbling down. Looking back now on those last fifteen months of her life I do so not with a deep ache of unresolved sadness, but with a remarkable and inexplicable sense of joy.

Of course it is painful to think that in this life I will never see her again. It is painful to think that we could have had so many more wonderful shared experiences together. It is painful to read her emails again and realise that we missed out on so much simply because we didn't know how to talk openly, and so we just kept quiet.

But we did forgive one another, and we were reconciled.

***

'Silas, I have a problem,' she said as we sat down for breakfast at the Brasserie in Old Brompton Road, London. 'I've been offered a good job, but if I take it, it means that I will have to lie to people, and I don't want to do that any more. I want to be a speaker of truth.' Julie said these words to me in the early summer of 2006. Two months later I was listening to an inspiring speaker telling a youth gathering of about 10,000 people that they ought to learn Arabic and use that language to promote peace in the Middle East. I got a recording of the talk and sent it to Julie. 'I've found you the perfect job, Julie, for when you are rid of the cancer. You have amazing experience of the Middle East and foreign affairs, and this role would enable you to speak the truth.' She asked me to send her more details. Within five months she was dead.

***

I was standing at the front of the church in Healaugh where people had crammed in to pay their respects to Julie. I was due to sing a song called 'Blessed Be Your Name'. This was

293

a song from a CD that Julie had requested I make for her. It was a happy-clappy song, but she liked it. It was playing on the CD player in her room at the time of her death nine days earlier. The second verse of the song goes like this:

> *Blessed be Your name when the sun's shining down*
> *on me,*
> *When the world is all that it should be, blessed be*
> *Your name*
> *Blessed be Your name, on the road marked with*
> *suffering*
> *When there is pain in the offering, blessed be Your*
> *name.*

I had been struggling to keep it together throughout the funeral service and now was the moment that I was going to be really exposed. 'Can we switch the two verses please?' I said to my friends Anna and Russel. 'You sing the first verse and I will sing the second. It'll give me a chance to get going.' All day it had been overcast and windy. But as I sang the lines printed above, a shaft of sunlight suddenly enveloped the church. In the days that followed her funeral I received a few letters. It wasn't just me who had noticed the shaft of sunlight. Another person asked me whether I had been aware of a beautiful white butterfly that had appeared over the congregation during the singing of that verse. Truly we were not alone that day.

You Can Die from That
Mary Crawley (II)

Chemotherapy is desperate and awful and she felt so ill with it. I remember once going to the doctor with her. She had said to me that she just couldn't go through another lot. I think there is a point with that treatment that you say 'I've had enough'. Doctors in those days were pretty unapproachable. But Julie had an extraordinary power or influence that intrigued people. This doctor had said I think you ought to do so and so. She said, 'I'm not going to have that.' I thought 'Oh my goodness me. What on earth is going to happen?' But the doctor, who was quite a difficult man, said, 'And why not?' She said, 'You can die from that.' So he didn't prescribe whatever it was. That was Julie – quietly, she knew her own mind. On the top, you would think she might be quite easy, but she was strong underneath.

She had a great sense of humour and she was a jolly person to meet. She did things that were very brave. She had a lot of friends who have been very supportive and generous all through the years. I think she was an engaging person whom people found very intriguing.

Good Work Completed
Priscilla Smith (III)

It was six years later that ill health struck again. One evening she called in to see me. 'The cancer has come back. It is in the bowel. I am going into hospital first thing in the morning and will be in for about ten days. I am telling the children that I am going away. They are not to know. Nor are Mummy or Daddy. I will be back up and running before Christmas.' Christmas was in two weeks' time. I could not sleep well that night but the verses that I read in my evening devotional said two things: 'He who has begun a good work in you will bring it to completion', and 'Carry one another's burdens'.

So, for the two weeks before Christmas, the children all staying with me, I carried a heavy secret. I let the nanny Paula into my confidence, as I needed to see Julie in hospital without anyone knowing where I was. Each afternoon I would slope off on some errand and drive to the centre of Leeds to persuade my recalcitrant sister that to keep our parents in the dark was not either kind or feasible. On the first afternoon, I arrived to find her asleep, but sitting up in the chair beside her bed, determined to push her body to get better quicker. There was a lot of blood; her sheets were dirty; on the table were a champagne bottle and glasses, and flowers gasping for water. The curtains were drawn to keep the nurses away. I changed the bed linen and cleaned up and got her back into a more comfortable position before trying to persuade her to be more realistic. I also discovered more about her medical condition from the nurses – it was not good: stage C bowel cancer – D is the worst – prognosis not great – chemotherapy following the operation. Grim prospects.

Julie was home for Christmas, albeit rather weary and fragile. The colostomy was eventually reversed (although she even hunted with the bag) and she embarked upon a treatment which was entirely diet- and food-related as she did not want to go through any more debilitating hospitalisation with the children around. It was a brave decision and for another six years she lived a really good life, eating organically, juicing endlessly, and, with the help of a kind dietary nurse called Dawn Mellor, she was soon clear of the cancer. She felt well, was energetic, and hunted at every opportunity. She was courageous in the extreme.

But one summer's day in 2005 she came, coughing, into the schoolroom at our house. She said that the cancer had returned – to her lungs. She had told Mummy and was going back to the doctor the next day. At least this time the burden would be shared. But the children were not to know. Nick, Silas and I began to talk.

The relationship between Julie and Daddy, with whom she now was easy and respectful, was better; but with Mummy it was bad, strained on both sides. We determined that in order to pray for physical healing we first had to heal relationships – so we prayed for the healing of the rift between Julie and Mummy and all of us. It was the distance and the biting words and the ridicule that we all felt so keenly. The boys had largely absented themselves as they found her scathing remarks so hard to bear, but the stakes were too high now. Nick came up from Sheffield on a very regular basis, befriending and talking to her, building confidence again. It was brave as they had had a bad row over Dominique many years previously, but Julie and Nick were very similar and they soon mended their fences. Meanwhile, Julie's health was getting worse. She had a very distended arm which was causing her a lot of pain. She was also struggling with the chemotherapy.

Silas had become friends with a couple from Seattle who had a healing ministry, which revolved around praying through and discerning God's purpose for our individual lives. It just so happened that they were in London on a day when Julie was going south for a second opinion on her arm. She had a couple of hours with them one December evening. They believe that no matter what we have done in the past, if we are to confess, acknowledge and forgive, all can be restored and a new freedom found. Julie was able to deal with some really difficult things that had hitherto tormented her. On that day, she found a new and profound freedom: gradually and imperceptibly at first, her manner changed, the biting tongue was more gentle, the humour kinder, the defences came down, the faith grew and to my utter joy she and I became close in a way that I had longed for all my life. We began really to talk and to share and to support each other.

In January, the size of the tumour in her arm bone made it break, causing her huge pain. It never got better. On 6 January, Daddy drove her to the hospital for an appointment and she had a fit and passed out in the car. We feared a brain tumour, and the weekend was anxious as we tried to both visit her and keep a semblance of normality for the children.

On Sunday evening I slipped off alone to see Julie. I was nervous as she had always fought shy of any form of 'God bothering', as Aunt Lish used to call it. We had a good chat, spoke some honest truths about her situation, and then I put my hand on her arm and prayed for God's healing power. 'Thank you,' she said simply. They were the same two words that she had written to me many years earlier in response to an honest letter of mine when there was a crisis over Rory Knight Bruce. I knew it meant a lot.

As I left the hospital, knowing that she really was very ill, I found myself grinning from ear to ear. My heart was full of joy. I was bemused and wondered what was going on. Driving back, I became overwhelmed with a sense of the power of the Holy Spirit and found myself in a state akin to what St Paul called speaking in tongues. The experience continued for the next forty minutes until I arrived home when it calmed down. Whatever it was, I knew that God was doing something and that I could be at peace. I decided to tell no one about what had happened and watch and see.

A scan the next day revealed that Julie had large brain tumours and that chemotherapy was necessary. On 10 January, the York & Ainsty (South) came for a lawn meet at her house. When it was all over, we stood in the kitchen and she fixed her eye on me and asked, 'Do you believe that God can heal me?' I evaded her gaze. I thought, well Daddy does; Nick is uncertain; and Silas thinks he might ... But what of me ... It was a hard question and I realised that my faith was lacking.

This crisis brought us together, and all historical barriers were abandoned. The boys came up from Bristol and, with her on a chair in the middle, all six of us sat in her sitting room to ask God to save her life. Many tears were shed. Our position was uncomfortable: Julie had resisted all things spiritual and never spoke with emotion of anything godly. From then on we laid hands on her and prayed for her every day. The effect was nothing short of miraculous and she immediately began to gather strength. By the end of March the scans showed that there was a tiny tumour left in the brain and that the lungs and liver were almost clear. Only the large arm remained. We would measure it to see if it was shrinking, but it remained a firm ten inches every time.

Julie got better. She even hunted once with her broken arm (terrifying even for her), protecting her emaciated bottom from saddle sores with a cushion. She began to work again, travelling a little, and engaged in discussions about becoming a peace envoy in the Middle East. She said she longed to find a job without subterfuge so that the years of deception could come to an end. But come the summer a scan revealed that the tumours were returning. The doctor advised against her going to Maine for the annual summer holiday, but she did not listen. The children still did not know how ill she really was: she kept her pecker up when they were around. Fynn got through his 'A' levels without seemingly realising the extent of her struggles and Letty was happily settled in her first year at Marlborough. Fynn drove himself and Lettice most of the long journeys back and forth from school. He was unlicensed; Julie bent the rules to suit her situation and took risks when she considered it to be necessary.

Julie collapsed on their return from Maine and I left our family holiday in Scotland for twenty-four hours to see her. It was the lowest point in our marriage as the family struggled with the drain that her illness was on all our lives. From that time on I fed her and looked after her most days, drawing strength from her own determination.

The summer over, Fynn set off for Australia, Letty returned to school and Julie retired to bed. She was determined that Fynn should not be restricted because of her health, but it was agony for her to let him go. She only agreed that if she was ill when they were around she would tell them the truth. Amazingly, she always rallied at half terms and weekends. In between it was grim, and she struggled with her sight, headaches and the interminable ache in her arm. She lay in bed with her arm resting on a mohair scarf and her head back against the pillows, listening to the World Service when reading was too much. She answered calls, wrote letters and worked away at relationships. She did not really want to see anyone and found the calls of people tiring, but was endlessly good-humoured and grateful, and we talked, prayed and worked things through together.

Julie was determined to reconcile with those with whom she had had hard times. She wrote letters forgiving people, said sorry to others and sought to make amends. Her decline over those autumn months was steady and when Fynn returned from Australia for a brief visit, he said, 'I'm not going back.' We both knew what that meant. He was devoted to his mother and spent most of the next six weeks sitting at the end of her bed on the little red sofa reading or working on his computer.

The days came and went, and the hospital visits were increasingly exhausting. She was taking a lot of steroids which caused her face to swell; deceptively, she did not look gaunt – the telltale sign was her nose, which was very thin. Becoming very weak, she spent longer each day in bed, often not getting up at all. Lettice came home for Christmas and she rallied again. Still there was no mention of the reality of the situation, but on Christmas Day when we gathered in church Lettice told a member of the congregation that she had given Mummy a very special stocking as it might be her last. Watching her walk up the aisle in a thick coat with her wig slightly askew, the telltale nose giving away her true condition, was a moving moment. We had a happy day all together at Healaugh and much laughter over lunch. Oliver and Julie bonded over politics and the grandparents were happy. The brothers came, and then wonderful Brigitte and Christopher, Ishbel and Catherine arrived to stay for New Year. The next morning I got the dreaded telephone call: Julie had collapsed. She never got out of bed again. Lettice had her birthday on 4 January and went back to school, but once she had gone, the downward spiral accelerated and by the 8th or so Julie could hardly speak. We looked first for carers but the process was slow and it was the Marie Curie nurses who formed the last reinforcements.

I had never given up hope that God could miraculously cure Julie. So one year almost to the day since Julie had eyeballed me and asked me about the depth of my faith, Silas and I agreed that he would come up and we would pray through the night for her healing. The day that we waited for Silas – until he arrived I felt like I was holding her life in my hands – was the day of the annual meet in Healaugh. It was ghastly weather: the wind howled, the rain lashed down, and it was dark and dreary. Late in the afternoon the fox tore through the garden, followed closely but vainly by the huntsman and the hounds, baying farewell as they went. It was as if the world and the heavens were fighting for her life. I had telephoned Letty to say that she needed to come home, and Silas brought her up with Jessie. The minutes seemed to drag as I longed for the time to pray. Daddy had come in to say goodbye and had spoken over her the poignant words, 'Until the shadows lengthen and the evening comes, and the busy world is hushed, and the fever of life is over ...' He then sat on the little red sofa with his head in his hands and wept. Mummy sat with her alone all afternoon, a time of healing that only a mother and daughter can know. It was the moment of reconciliation long awaited. But still Silas did not come.

At last, late on, they arrived. At Catherine's suggestion, we gave Julie communion. One by one the others left to go to bed and Silas and I set out for our all-night vigil. But instead of my planned plea to God for a miracle, I found that I could only thank Him for all that He had done in her life, for all that she had achieved, all that she had shown us, all that God had done for her, all that I had learnt through her life. After a while Silas and I both lifted our heads and agreed that we needed to stop. He went to bed and I sat up with her during the night.

The Marie Curie nurses had called for the district nurse and the doctor to come and fit her with a morphine drip as she was in so much pain. The medical team eventually converged on the doorstep. The out-of-hours doctor came from Harrogate, the ambulance came from York and the district nurse came from Leeds. They stood at the door discussing whose responsibility it was to be there, who should do the fitting, and which hospital authority was in the wrong. Julie had spent months working for the hospital trust, and I am sure that she was rocking with laughter within her comatose state. Mercifully they decided to put their differences aside, so the pain relief was finally installed and Julie was more comfortable. At seven in the morning Silas came to relieve me and I left for some sleep. 'We have to let her go,' he said.

Sleep was fitful and a little later I took our younger two down to say goodbye to her; she was peaceful. Mummy and the Marie Curie nurse were there all morning, and Lettice and Fynn were with her. At about one p.m. the telephone rang. 'Come quickly please,' said Catherine, 'she is going.' As I drove those few minutes to the house I noticed that the sun was shining and it was crisp and clear. Everyone was gathered around her bed. 'Thank you,' I said, and kissed her, and then she was gone. Those two words again. It was all that needed to be said.

As we stood and wept, I heard the words of the song that was playing on the compilation of worship that she had asked Silas to make for her, 'You give and take away, you give and take away, my heart will choose to say blessed be the Lord.' It was as if God were speaking to us. Laid there, she looked so peaceful and utterly serene – all the anxiety gone. Truly she was beautiful. We laid lilies on her and savoured the moments at her side. Ali arrived soon after and we searched out one of her many cameras to take photographs of her, but ironically none came out. It was too precious a moment to record.

But it was the dogs who had the last laugh. As the Marie Curie nurses laid her out, her faithful canine friends Harry and Sally determinedly lay like sentinels, unmoving, at the foot of the bed. Later, we were still trying to take photographs when the undertakers came to take her body away, so we asked them to wait in the stairwell. But there was dog poo on the stairs; someone had trodden in it in the garden and brought it up with them. Out went Mr Barker Junior in his coat and tails to clean his shoes. How Julie would have laughed.

When people reflect on her life, many say how unfair it was that she should have suffered so much. But I think just the opposite. Time and again her life was threatened, whether by riding, by war, by dangerous people or by the three cancers. Her life could have been taken at any one of those times. But she was preserved, for she had a job to do. Some months after her death I opened the Psalms again. The emotion had been too raw for me to deal with before then, but now I read these words: 'All the days ordained for me were written in your book before one of them came to be' (Psalm 139:14) and 'He who has begun a good work in you has brought it to completion.'

EPILOGUE

EPILOGUE

Epilogue
Lettice Crawley Peck

My mother was extraordinary. Beautiful, exasperating, whip-sharp and wildly opinionated, she captured the love and loyalty of all who met her.

She was generous with her gifts and her trust, relying on her own intuition over the opinions of others. Integrity was vital and she had no patience for fools – something she often made all too evident.

This book – and this entry – is not a glorification of her virtues – no doubt she would roll her eyes – 'darling, *really*!' – hiding, perhaps, a pleased little grin. However, it is only with hindsight, and the later discoveries that I made about how difficult her life really was, that I can fully appreciate what an unusually brave and unique person she was.

She was a glorious blend of opposites: militant about honesty, she would lie furiously about her age: '*I'm twenty-six, darling!*' she would hiss if ever I announced the truth. Periodically, she would concede, and update her age, but never in line with the calendar year, and only when I forced the more dubious mathematics of my existence upon her.

As a parent, she encouraged wild abandon, survival of the fittest, and strict moral code. She used to delight in our eccentricity, allowing us to dress however we chose, with often – in my case at least – bizarre results. She considered

Fynn and me her minions, useful at dinner parties – 'Oh *don't* bother washing up, the children will do it' – and a free furniture rearrangement service. We were regularly enlisted to redistribute awkwardly shaped furniture – the jukebox, a throne or treasure chest from Pakistan, an Afghan cupboard originally designed to hold Qur'ans that was used as a drinks cabinet. These would be relocated around the house by Fynn and me at her whim. Often, within five minutes, we were told to take them back. Knowing her sense of humour, much of this was probably done to wind us up – a sort of perverse session of family bonding – something she was very keen on.

Winding us up was something she took great pleasure in. I was given a reading in church one Christmas, and I went to her, unsure how to pronounce a word. 'Pig-ee-on', she told me, with a grin. Years of merciless teasing followed. My cousins lived in the same village, and the eldest, Verena, who is my age, was an annoyingly helpful child. I was regularly reminded of this. 'Lettice, do the washing up. I bet you Priscilla doesn't have to ask Verena to do the washing up – I bet you Verena just does it. Why can't you be more like *Verena*?' Once, furious at the endless unfavourable comparisons, I shot back: 'If you think Verena's so fantastic why don't you swap us!' She considered this for a moment. 'Well darling, I would, but I don't think Priscilla would want *you*.' In the same way, whenever I believed that I was being given more chores than Fynn, and demanded why, her response was usually: 'Because he's the favourite.'

This was a prevailing theme with which she often used to tease me. Once, aged about seven, I was told to do the washing up. 'Fynn the favourite', was provided as the reason. I declared in a fury that I was running away. My mother didn't bat an eyelid. Full of righteous indignation, I packed a small rucksack and stormed out of the house. I think I remember that she even waved me off with a cheerful, 'Bye, darling.'

I got as far as a mud den that Fynn and I had made in a shrub at the end of our horse paddock and sat, seething at the perceived injustice. Gloatingly, I picturing her worried face as time passed and I didn't return. I imagined her wringing her hands, calling the police and cursing herself for treating me so unfairly. Telling Fynn that I was in fact the favourite. After what I thought was several hours but was probably at most forty-five minutes, I got cold, and, not hearing any police sirens, trudged home. I slunk inside, expecting that my mother would at least dash towards me with open arms. Not a bit. I bumped into her somewhere in the house a few minutes later. She raised an eyebrow. 'I thought you were running away?' I glared at her. 'I've come back.' She pulled a disappointed face, then brightened. 'Well there's still the washing up!'

It becomes clear, the more I reflect upon our lives together, that my mother had great fun with us. She had certain catch-phrases that she would trot out right when she knew it was most annoying. If we were playing a board game, Risk, or Monopoly, and one of us was losing (we are both terrible losers) she would sidle over and with a serene, knowing smile advise us to 'go down with our flags flying'. 'Share, share with a smile,' she would chant, grinning, as we battled over coveted possessions.

Like many parents, she thrilled at embarrassing us. At sports events at my local Yorkshire prep school she would make no secret of the fact that she thought coming to watch the 'C' team (I really wasn't very good) a complete waste of time. When she did turn up, it was often worse. I have painful memories of her bellowing impatiently from the side-lines, 'Come on, darling! Get those fat legs pumping!' or, 'Just *hit* them, darling!'

'You *can't* Mother, it's hockey!' I would scream back across the field.

'*Of course you can. Just be subtle about it!*'

This humour came with discipline. Once, aged about nine, I pestered her so much in the car driving home that she threatened to kick me out if I didn't stop immediately. I didn't believe her – we were half a mile from home, and continued. Sure enough I was booted out and left to walk the rest of the way.

These stories may paint a picture of terrible parenting – indeed, in moments of deep irritation I would snap, '0800 11 11 Mother. *Childline*.' She would whip back, 'There should be a Parentline, far more useful!'

Yet despite her edges, she was also soft, and deeply kind. I was too young, at fifteen, to fully appreciate this – she had a moral compass locked on north, and the willingness to pause, and act, if she saw an injustice. She was never one to turn guiltily from an unpleasant sight or cross the street to avoid the homeless. Although at times she could be a terrible snob – she refused to let me out of the house in trainers, and often habits or things I picked up from my local Yorkshire prep school were outlawed as 'hoipolloi' – she had friends from all walks of life. She treated everyone with the same easy charm, and was just as at home with local farmers and runaway children as she was with exotic strangers and aristocrats, all of whom passed regularly through the house in Yorkshire.

It is worth describing this house, which brimmed with eccentricity. Three cottages glued together on the outskirts of a village in Yorkshire, it was a far cry from my mother's previous lives in Pakistan and Russia. Instead, she filled the rooms with furniture and treasures from all over the world – I have mentioned some above, but there was so much more. Our dining room was a memorial to old Russia: it was painted communist red and original propaganda posters showing workers striding through factories and fields covered the walls, while a giant stone bust of Lenin's head sat on the window sill. One wall of the drawing room was filled by a painting of

Mummy....
Will you be my

Generous

Nice

Cool

Fashionable

UNembarrassing

Rule Abiding

Loving

Fair

Mother gor ever?

A hopeful letter, copying her father's, written to her mother by Lettice, aged about seven

the storming of the Winter Palace in St Petersburg, and books on politics in Turkmenistan wrestled for space with Mills & Boon and Anthony Trollope. We had knives everywhere, a machete in the sitting room, Afghan daggers stuffed away in drawers, and a pistol in her sock drawer. An Afghan cot served as a coffee table, cupboards were crammed with ornate Russian teapots and gold Venetian goblets, and rugs from all over the Middle East lined the floors. And throughout the years, the same music playing from the jukebox and the drawing room: Leonard Cohen, Eartha Kitt, Bob Dylan and the Rolling Stones were the soundtrack of my childhood.

Always, there were animals, and her approach to them was as laissez-faire as it was to her children. We were all left much to our own devices, let out to play in the morning, and if you returned in the evening, well that was fine too. In Pakistan, there was a monkey, a parrot and a donkey; in Russia, mostly horses. In Yorkshire, we had a steady stream of dogs, horses, cats, goldfish, terrapins, budgies. There was an alarmingly high turnover of all – particularly the budgies, whose mysterious, and almost monthly demise we eventually discovered was down to the smoke from burnt toast. At this, my mother stopped replacing them. She was not one to bother hunting round for replicas to spare our feelings. The goldfish lived in a murky water trough in the horse field, where they were completely forgotten, until one day I decided to clean it out, and discovered that they still existed, and had grown abnormally large and black.

We had many dogs, mostly rescue ones. When we lost one – as we frequently did – to a rabbit hole, death, or thieves from Leeds – she would go to the RSPCA and pick the dog which had been there the longest. Dogs are given fourteen weeks there before they are put down, and it was an act of great kindness to save some of the older, uglier ones from this. Harry and Sally were her favourites, a small gruff terrier which lived up to its name and terrorised (and sometimes killed) the local cats, and a soft golden lurcher which would patiently ignore the chaos around her. We had two cats, Sooty, and my own splendid giant of a Maine Coon cat, Finnegan, which she gave me for my twelfth birthday. Sooty – aptly named, as it turned out – made the local headlines for his miraculous survival of our house fire, in which a fireman resuscitated him with a ventilator and CPR. The local newspaper headline read the next day: 'Tadcaster cat: nine lives'. Such are the excitements of village life.

Her greatest passion was horses, of which she had many, never quite having the heart to sell them. She was a phenomenal rider, and totally fearless in the saddle. Her favourite was Light Brownie, a gorgeous stallion she saved from the knackers' yard in Russia, and brought back to England in full Muscovite headdress. Riding was a big part of my childhood, and she would take me out hunting, first on my fat little Shetland Sparky – for which she would grudgingly take me on a lead rein, until she could fob me off on someone else and race to the front of the field. Hunting etiquette was highly important, and she insisted that I always carried a full hipflask of sloe gin to offer round. This made us both immensely popular with the local hunt, who completely adored her. She wore a smart Patey hat, and was scathing of body protectors – considering them 'for wimps'.

Once, shortly before my eleventh birthday, she organised a hunt meet at our house. A few days later, she asked me guiltily, 'Your birthday's on the eighth of January, darling, isn't it?' I laughed, thinking she was joking, and reminded her it was the fourth. Pause. 'Ah.' As it turned out, the meet was on the fourth, and I was drafted in to serve food and join the hunt. At this point I loathed hunting as I had a particularly difficult pony and by midday was crying with rage, having been thrown off twice.

Although she had expensive tastes, she was equally at home on a camel in the desert or camping by the lakes of North America. She loved caviar, yet would regularly remind us that 'sell-by dates are a con', as she scraped layers of mould from cheese or jam. At Marlborough events she would arrive with rice cakes and a couple of slightly mouldy apples – a far cry from the hampers laden with houmous and chocolate that was standard fare at such events. I was ordered to fend for myself.

Style. Above all, it was clear that my mother had style. In her life, her attitude, and her wardrobe – she carried herself in a way that meant you couldn't help but admire her. She wore her patch with panache, and it added to her air of danger and adventure. Her wardrobe was an expensive mix of black leather trousers, men's shirts, tiger-print Versace, kitten heels and floor-length fur coats. One can imagine the impression she made in the sleepy Yorkshire countryside.

Relaxing on a boat in Maine with some light reading

Many of my memories of her are in Maine, our family home in America, which we visited for weeks on end every year. Hordes of cousins were invited, and these were the happiest weeks of the summer. For her, the house was a sanctuary, a place to remember my father and escape the pressures of normal life. It is in Maine that I now feel her and remember her most strongly. Every piece of furniture has a memory attached, and Nora Jones played on year after year. It was a house of industry, every year there was some task to be done, we built docks, painted tables and repanelled walls.

It was in Maine that I learned to water-ski. We went out on to the lake with my uncle, and after various unsuccessful attempts at getting up, she had the not-so-brilliant idea of tying my skis together (fine), and to the boat (more dubious). I was understandably reluctant, but was reassured with a breezy, 'It's fine darling, I'll watch you, and as soon as you fall over we'll stop.' The boat started up again. I fell. Unfortunately, she had already turned away to take photos of something else, and failed to notice as I was dragged along behind the boat. Of course when she did realise, and stopped, there was no apology.

Such was her parenting. Near-death experiences were dismissed as 'character building', and expressions of sympathy at misfortunes were rarely forthcoming: Fynn drilling through his thumb, my breaking my leg, one of us launching war upon the other, all elicited the same response: a raised eyebrow, and the advice that we should 'get on with it'. 'Don't be a telltale-tit,' she would reply if Fynn yelled as I sat behind him in the car and pulled his hair, 'she's just trying to annoy you – don't rise to it.' Often her advice came with an anecdote of how such a thing had happened to her (only worse) and she had, of course, remained stoically silent.

Annoyingly, she was often right. She was extraordinarily brave, and expected the same of us. Once, she broke her pelvis in a riding accident. She lay, stubborn and bedridden, for three days until she was forced by my grandmother to go to hospital.

Her stoicism was one of her most memorable features. It must have seemed at times as though the universe was testing her. Tragedy and misfortune rolled in like an endless storm for much of her life, battering her resolve, waiting for a hairline fissure to open up, for her to crack and break down. Yet she never did, and more than that, she was so much more than her circumstances.

Not once do I remember seeing her cry, through pain, physical or otherwise, or loneliness. Even at the end, when her pain must have been excruciating, she smiled through it. What's more, her life – our lives – were not defined by past tragedies, or present illness. By giving us such an example, our mother equipped us as best she could for the future – a future she knew she would not be part of.

Thus, despite what might seem to be an advert for how to drive your child to therapy, I had a wonderfully happy childhood. This in itself is a tribute to her courage – for although she had cancer for many of our fifteen years together, through a mixture of her stoicism, my childish self-absorption, and perhaps a large dose of denial on both of our parts, her illness seemed to have little place in our lives until the very latter years.

Shortly before her death, when her left arm had swollen from a broken bone and the cancer surrounding it, she suggested the idea to us that she might have it amputated, and we laughed about her getting a hook and parrot to match the patch that covered the loss of her eye ten years previously. I spent many a night in her bed, re-watching *Bridget Jones' Diary* and *Legally Blonde* (our two favourite films), and trying not-so-subtly to read the diaries that she was forever writing. Needless to say, her watchful eye and appalling calligraphy kept me from catching anything of interest.

I would plead, 'But *when* can I read them, Mummy?' Her response: a wry, 'When I'm dead.'

She went to great lengths to hide her illness, resting for weeks on end only to leap out of bed when we came home from boarding school for a few days. Other times she would tell us she was on holiday, when in fact she was in hospital. Away at school the other side of the country, I was blind to the reality of her deterioration. On my birthday, a week before she died, I was taken back to school. I remember rushing into her room to say goodbye, and her cheerful smile. If you had asked, right then, I would have told you she was going to be fine.

As each year passes the memories fade. This book marks ten years since her death, and it is only with distance and a little more maturity that I can fully appreciate how wonderful she really was. At every milestone in life, my exams, leaving school, university, I imagine her commentary. 'You flunked Drama GCSE? Not a proper subject. I *told* you to do Latin.' 'Edinburgh, darling – just like me! Only the best people go to Edinburgh. *Cleaver* girl.'* She lived a life seemingly cursed by continual misfortune with style and courage, cramming a hundred years of adventures into forty-six. Some of those adventures have been recorded here, and her vivacity, charm and strength shine through in every story.

* A family joke after I miswrote 'clever' on a card for Fynn.

LAST WORD:
LETTER TO *THE TIMES*
6 May 1998

From Mrs Rory Peck

Sir,

Canvassing for the Tadcaster West ward in a Selby District Council by-election, I struck up a conversation with a local pensioner. She asked me which party I was standing for and when I told her the Conservatives, she replied: 'Oh my dear, I know just how you feel. I'm a Jehovah's Witness.'

Yours sincerely,

Juliet Peck

York Road Mews,
Healaugh,
North Yorkshire
LS24 8DD

Juliet at York Road Mews, Healaugh